NAVIGATING *to* JESUS

A JOURNEY OF FAITH

NAVIGATING *to* JESUS

A JOURNEY OF FAITH

AARON & JULIE BUJNOWSKI

CFI
An imprint of Cedar Fort, Inc.
Springville, Utah

Paperback ISBN 13: 978-1-4621-4997-1
eBook ISBN 13: 978-1-4621-4998-8

Published by CFI, an imprint of Cedar Fort, Inc.
2373 W. 700 S., Suite 100, Springville, UT 84663
Distributed by Cedar Fort, Inc., www.cedarfort.com

Library of Congress Cataloging Number: 2025938892

Cover design by Shawnda Craig

Printed in the United States of America

10 9 8 7 6 5 4 3 2 1

Printed on acid-free paper

For Breanna and Liam

CONTENTS

PREFACE

THE ANSWER IS ALWAYS JESUS

There is no other way nor means whereby [we] can be saved, only through the atoning blood of Jesus Christ. . . . Remember that he cometh to redeem the world.

—HELAMAN 5:9

Life as a covenant disciple of Jesus Christ is beautiful. We believe that we are spirit offspring of loving heavenly parents. We understand God's plan of mercy for His children, the center of which is our Savior, Jesus Christ. We relish the abundant grace and mercy Jesus offers, which allow us to be imperfect, yet through willing repentance, to become perfected through Him. We experience deep spiritual joys and have access to His precious eternal promises. We can feel an enhanced and eternal sense of purpose and a great love for God and all His children, which leads us to do much good in this life as we seek to emulate Christ. Throughout our life of faithful Christian discipleship, we experience stages of spiritual, mental, and emotional growth that enable us to become more like our heavenly parents. For a disciple of Jesus Christ, mortality is our road back to God.

Unfortunately, life itself is often hard. Every individual who has lived on this planet has experienced some type of difficulty or challenge, and disciples of Jesus Christ are no exception. As His disciples, we face pain, sickness, unfairness, trauma, abuse, loss, and myriad other heartbreaking experiences—just like every other person. Our faith in Jesus does not prevent pain.

Furthermore, we can experience periods of doubt where our faith and loyalty are stretched, sometimes to breaking points. Notwithstanding their ubiquity, mortality's frequent and often intense difficulties can provide us with some of our most enriching experiences. A great paradox of mortality is that we spiritually grow the most when we face our toughest challenges. Our eternal progress depends on mortal difficulty. The extent and nature of our progress and whether we feel joy despite challenges depend on our choices and not our circumstances.

OUR JOURNEY OF FAITH

Like all couples, our married life together has not been without trouble. We have experienced some of the most heart-wrenching events imaginable. Some have occurred randomly due to life's circumstances. Other events have occurred due to the actions of others—some of which were specifically directed at one or both of us. Unfortunately, these negative experiences have occurred outside *and* inside of The Church of Jesus Christ of Latter-day Saints. The source, setting, and type of our difficulties aren't as important as their effect on us. The pain is real.

Regardless of our multiple challenges, we feel blessed to have been able to move forward positively even when our issues were not resolved as we wanted—or at all. Looking back, this outcome is miraculous. Betrayal, maliciousness, and vindictiveness should have caused us to stop trusting others. Unfairness, misfortune, and calamity should have caused us to lose trust in God. Yet trust remained. Even more miraculously, love for God and others grew.

We are not perfect. These events sometimes caused us to question and doubt many things. We shed tears and hurled complaints. We were deeply disappointed. We even felt anger and bitterness. But when the hard came (and it always comes), we pushed forward until it had no more power over us. Sometimes, we found a resolution. Other times, we found a greater ability to cope with a problem that had no solution. In either case, the difficulties dissipated, and we emerged a little better than before; a little humbler, a bit more loving, incrementally more patient, and kinder. Peace returned until the next hard thing emerged, and the process repeated.

We have often talked about why this pattern of progress occurred in our lives. We've tried to find a common factor to identify why trust, love, and kindness always overcame fear, hatred, and anger. Of the many things that may have fueled our forward motion,[1] one stood out above the rest. For us, this path has been a journey of faith, faith in Jesus Christ, our foundation.

Why faith? At its core, faith means that some things remain unknown, and we move forward anyway. Faith in Jesus means that we look to Him for guidance when we don't know our next step forward. We seek for comfort from Him when our hearts are breaking. We trust in His purposes when we can't find meaning in the difficult events we experience. And if the hard does not dissipate or the consequences are not removed, we remain loyal to Him anyway. Faith in Jesus is an active loyalty to Him, notwithstanding what we don't yet know.

We recognize that many others have not found solace in their faith in Jesus. In fact, their faith may have been compromised due to the hard. We also recognize that non-believers may also get through their challenges in other ways, unrelated to a Christian faith, and can still find outcomes that are positive. We are happy for their successes and in no way seek to diminish all they have accomplished through personal effort and the support of loving friends and family.

However, we feel compelled to testify of Jesus Christ and how our faith in Him enabled us to deal with our hard times and still find joy in Him and His gospel. If His eternal promises are true—and we witness that they are—then the full effect of our faith journey will not only be experienced in this life, but we will also see that joy amplified in the next. We might suggest that this eternal hope is worth remaining true to Him.

This book is written to all who are on a journey of faith. You may have just started your journey and are looking for meaning and purpose in life, not yet having experienced God. You may be early in your journey of faith, having recently covenanted with Jesus at baptism. Alternatively, you may be an experienced disciple of Jesus Christ with many enriching, faith-filled experiences, and you want to deepen your faith in Him. Some of you may be in a faith crisis, where unknowns and doubts are causing you to question why you even believed to begin with. Wherever you are on your journey of faith, we wrote this book for you.

We share the principles in this book to help you navigate to Jesus while on your faith journey. Why Jesus? President Russell M. Nelson has taught,

> The joy we feel has little to do with the circumstances of our lives and everything to do with the focus of our lives. When the focus of our lives is on God's plan of salvation . . . and Jesus Christ and His gospel, we can feel joy regardless of what is happening—or not happening—in our lives. Joy comes from and because of Him. He is the source of all joy.[2]

Through more than thirty years of marriage and over fifty years of living, we affirm with President Nelson that Jesus is the source of all joy. We know this truth by personal experience, and we want to help you find that same joy in Him through your life's experiences.

THE STAGES OF FAITH

Our faith in Jesus has grown and matured with time. This process of spiritual growth and maturing faith happened slowly throughout the course of our lives. Like vegetation that germinates from tiny seeds into sprouting seedlings and then grows to fully mature plants and trees, we also moved through defined stages of spiritual growth, each of which required a gradual change in our faith in Jesus Christ.

Likewise, all disciples of Christ progress through different stages of faith as we mature spiritually. Many astute and thoughtful people have studied this journey of faith and have created frameworks to describe the path.[3] Interestingly, the overarching processes different people describe are strikingly similar, despite variations in terminology and detail. As we researched these frameworks, we found one that resonated with us because it seemed to accurately describe our own faith journey. We also liked its simplicity, which may help better understand its concepts. The framework we share was created by author Brian McLaren. In his book, *Faith After Doubt*, McLaren proposes four stages of faith that define a person's spiritual growth journey:[4] simplicity, complexity, perplexity, and harmony (shown here).

Stages of Faith*

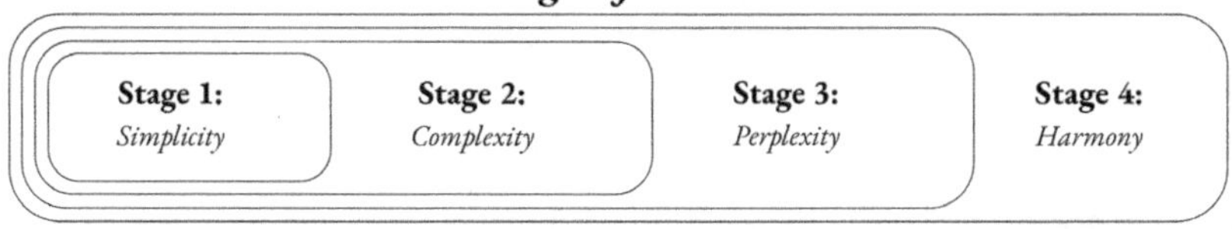

*"Stages of Faith" © Brian D. McLaren.

Regardless of the specific framework, understanding that faith stages occur and that everyone is progressing within and among them at different rates are keys to successfully navigating spiritual progress. As we understand this process, we will be better prepared to move through our own personal faith journey.

This comprehension may also enable us to avoid contention and confusion when we interact with others. Some conflicts of faith can arise because individuals are at different stages in their faith journey. They either don't understand the reality of the differences in themselves and others, or they don't give each other sufficient grace to grow and change. Empathy for others' spiritual progress will increase as our understanding of this process improves.

From our study, we came to understand that the stages of faith are not linear. They are progressive, like growth rings in a tree.[5] Later stages build upon and coexist with earlier stages. Thus, people may experience elements of multiple stages simultaneously, move back and forth between stages, or repeat a progression through the stages for different principles throughout their lives.

Spiritual growth requires change, and change is hard. The process can often be messy and filled with uncertainty. Individual experiences will vary.[6] However, we would suggest that a consistent feature of all spiritual growth and any faith journey is that movement within or among its stages requires the realization that where our faith is moving is different than where it has been. This insight can be both exhilarating and exhausting—for us and others.

With this introduction in mind, we'll describe in more detail each of the stages of faith presented by Brian McLaren.

SIMPLICITY[7]

The stage called *simplicity* is a childlike faith characterized by an understanding of religious or spiritual concepts that follows a well-defined framework. This stage involves accepting beliefs and teachings without significant questioning or critical analysis and rejecting anything outside of defined boundaries. For individuals in this stage, the difference between good and bad is clear. Right and wrong are well defined. Good always wins, and evil is always defeated. This stage is marked by a sense of trust, innocence, and heavy reliance on external authorities, such as parents, teachers, or Church leaders, for guidance and interpretation of their faith.

Many faithful Latter-day Saints and their fellow Christians choose to remain in this stage of growth. They find safety and security here. Remaining in this stage on any given principle or issue (or perhaps on all principles) can keep people away from spiritual danger. However, fixating on simplicity can also lead to becoming self-righteous and judgmental, especially of others who choose to wrestle with spiritual complexities they encounter as they move through mortality.

COMPLEXITY[8]

As individuals spiritually grow and develop, their faith becomes more complicated and nuanced. In the *complexity* stage, individuals begin to question previously held beliefs when they encounter information that doesn't fit their defined framework. This complexity can act as an opposition to their simplistic faith. They often explore and deepen their original understanding based on this new information, although some retreat to the simplicity stage to avoid dealing with emerging complexity.

In the best cases, the complexity stage involves critical thinking, personal reflection, deep study, sincere prayer, personal revelation, and an exploration of different perspectives and interpretations. Individuals begin to grapple with uncertainties and conflicts between their previously established views and their evolving understanding. They can become enthusiastic learners but must resist the trap of becoming overly confident. They turn to God for direct spiritual insight through prayer, and they often find their answers. Their seeking frequently gives way to new spiritual insights and greater strength. It can also be a gateway to further questioning, which leads to the next stage of faith.

PERPLEXITY[9]

The stage of *perplexity* occurs when individuals encounter profound questions, paradoxes, and challenges that shake their faith to its core. This situation may occur slowly as a person encounters greater complexity, but it can also be triggered by personal crises, intellectual or interpersonal conflicts, or other experiences that significantly challenge their previously held beliefs. For these issues, there do not seem to be answers, and God seems to remain silent when He is approached in prayer. This stage is usually characterized by a deep sense of doubt, uncertainty, and existential questioning. Individuals may feel spiritually disoriented or confused. They may even experience a crisis where their doubts overwhelm their faith.

Sadly, some give up on deeply held beliefs and walk away, never progressing to the final stage where their spiritual conflicts are resolved within the context of their belief system. As their critical thinking gives way to cynicism, some leave their current faith while others leave faith altogether. Faith abandonment often ends the immediate internal conflict, but it doesn't always bring lasting spiritual peace. In some cases, individuals may even openly fight against their previous faith or all people of faith, striving to draw others away with them in a misguided attempt to force their own perplexity upon others.[10] Unfortunately, social media amplifies these voices, giving them a broad platform to gather with other like-minded and perplexity-riddled individuals.

Fortunately, some people in the perplexity stage engage in intense soul-searching—a heartfelt quest to reexperience God and faith, explore their own or alternative spiritual paths, or seek guidance from mentors, counselors, or Church leaders. Prayers to God intensify and are sustained while waiting for guidance. For them, this deconstruction process breaks down previous narrow or even erroneous views and begins to rebuild faith with more profound or expansive insights. A strengthened and nuanced faith can emerge from this process.

Deconstruction is not destruction. Deconstruction is part of a rebuilding process. In the same way that remodeling a home requires the removal of unwanted structures such as walls and cabinets, remodeling faith often requires the removal or modification of old notions and viewpoints. This process happens to individuals who convert to the restored Church, leaving behind old religious understanding and habits and replacing them with new ones. The process should happen to all who remake themselves in the similitude of the Savior over the course of their mortal lives. This change is called *being born again* when the foundation upon which we build is Jesus Christ.

For determined Christians who work through perplexity, their strengths are their curiosity and ability to think critically while simultaneously keeping their hand on the iron rod of their original faith: Jesus Christ. This phase may last an extended period, requiring endurance and continued effort. Nevertheless, when pursued with purpose and patience, the reward is moving to the next phase of faith.

HARMONY[11]

The final stage of faith, *harmony*, is where individuals reconcile the complexities and perplexities of their faith journey and find true peace. They rediscover Jesus and have a renewed faith in Him. In cases where a resolution is not found, people accept unknowns and paradoxes, choosing to move forward anyway. They patiently wait upon God for answers to come in His way and time. These actions are the very definition of faith, and the perplexity they faced in the previous stage was the trial that provided the witness they sought.[12] This stage involves integrating newfound insights, experiences, paradoxes, divine guidance, and personal beliefs into a newly refined spiritual framework. Harmony is defined by an authentic sense of inner peace, acceptance, and alignment between their beliefs and experiences.

People in harmony no longer require external validation for their faith. They know for themselves.[13] Using restoration language, those in harmony are fully converted, having experienced a mighty change of heart.[14] They are born again with renewed spiritual strength.[15]

With this strong, renewed internal foundation, individuals often develop a more inclusive and expansive approach to their faith, appreciating the diversity and interconnectedness of various spiritual paths. In the best cases, they find solace in their original faith and experience a deepened connection with it while also respecting and appreciating the beliefs of others. They move forward with a refined framework to incorporate new information into their foundation of faith. Disciples of Jesus Christ and members of covenant Israel strengthen their witness of the Savior, having "overcome by faith" in Him.[16]

Harmony can appear very similar to simplicity. Individuals in the harmony stage have an unassuming confidence in their faith, not because they know everything but precisely because they know they *don't.* Yet they move forward anyway. This is faith. Their spiritual sophistication can appear straightforward, but inwardly their spirituality has multiple layers of depth born of well-considered information and oft-inspired wrestling. Their experiences beget wisdom and peace, two fruits of the torturous path they so painfully traversed.

GOD'S PATTERN OF FAITH

As we learned the concept of faith stages and pondered how we and others have navigated them successfully, we read numerous resources by authors of multiple faiths who have addressed the doubts and struggles associated with faith journeys. We found a tremendous amount of helpful information and counsel. Still, we wanted to find a well-articulated answer to this question: How do we move through our faith journey and remain true to the restored gospel and our covenants? We wanted to discover God's pattern in this process, yet the many resources we studied did not provide an entirely satisfactory answer. So we searched for our answer in the scriptures.

We reread the scriptures with our question in mind because, as Elder David A. Bednar taught, "The scriptures are full of spiritual patterns."[17] We tried to find a familiar framework—God's pattern of faith—that would answer our question. We read scriptural accounts from ancient and modern prophets, evaluating those canonized "case studies" of individuals who progressed through their stages of faith to reach a change of heart and a complete conversion to Jesus Christ. As we worked and sought the guidance of the Spirit, we discovered our answer.

We found God's divine pattern of faith while studying the Book of Mormon. Once we discovered it, we began to see the pattern in the lives of people in the scriptures, our own lives, and the lives of many others. We also realized that those who struggled on their faith journey were missing elements of this pattern. Here is God's pattern of faith and where we first discovered it.

During his final address to his people, King Benjamin describes an experience when an angel delivered to him a message testifying of the Redeemer. The angel's message was a powerful witness of Jesus Christ who would come to redeem the world from sin and death. This angelic message is one of the most powerful and specific prophecies of Christ recorded in scripture.[18] King Benjamin's vision of the Redeemer was our first and most important key: Jesus Christ must be the focus of any successful faith journey. We must navigate to Him if we are to successfully traverse our journey of faith.

After sharing his sacred and powerful experience, King Benjamin observes that his people had fallen to the earth, having viewed themselves in their fallen state. Expressing their sincere belief in the Savior and their deep desire to be redeemed, King Benjamin witnesses that they received a remission of their sins.[19]

At this point, King Benjamin describes the process of how their "mighty change" came about.[20] We realized that each event he describes in his summary of their conversion constitutes elements of God's pattern of faith—the way that we progress spiritually through our mortality and move through and within the stages of faith while remaining true to the Savior and His gospel. We summarize this pattern of how King Benjamin's people navigated to Jesus in the table that follows.[21]

Event Observed by King Benjamin	**God's Pattern of Faith**
"They had fallen to the earth, for the fear of the Lord had come upon them."[22]	Experience an Opposition
"The knowledge of God has awakened you to a sense of your nothingness."[23]	Awaken unto God

Event Observed by King Benjamin	God's Pattern of Faith
"Ye have come to a knowledge of the goodness of God . . . and also, the atonement which has been prepared from the foundation of the world."[24]	Know God's Plan of Mercy
"[The Atonement] is the means whereby salvation cometh ... there is none other salvation save this . . . neither are there any conditions whereby man [and woman] can be saved."[25]	Seek This Jesus
"Believe in God; believe that he is, and he created all things . . . believe that he has all wisdom, and all power . . . believe that man [and woman] doth not comprehend all the things which the Lord comprehend . . . believe that ye must repent of your sins."[26]	Just Believe on Him
"If ye believe all these things, see that ye do them. . . . If ye do this . . . ye shall grow."[27]	Act on Faith in Him
"I would that ye should remember, and always retain in remembrance, the greatness of God . . . and his goodness and long-suffering toward you . . . calling on the name of the Lord daily."[28]	Always Remember Him
"Always rejoice . . . and always retain a remission of your sins."[29]	Endure in Faith on His Name
"Love one another . . . serve one another . . . succor those that stand in need . . . administer of your substance unto him that standeth in need."[30]	Minister in His Love
"The Spirit of the Lord Omnipotent . . . has wrought a mighty change in us, or in our hearts, that we have no more disposition to do evil, but to do good continually. And we, ourselves, also, through the infinite goodness of God, and the manifestations of his Spirit, have great views of that which is to come."[31]	Witness a Mighty Change

After finding this pattern in King Benjamin's speech, we began to see it in the Book of Mormon and throughout all the standard works. Repeatedly, we saw the same pattern in the lives of scriptural characters. We also realized that we saw it in our own lives. Most importantly, we noticed a single thread that tied together all the pattern's principles: Jesus Christ.

JESUS IS THE WAY

The tie that binds together God's pattern of faith is Jesus. "In him all things hold together."[32] For this reason, God always focuses us on Jesus Christ and His infinite Atonement. "This is my beloved Son, hear him!" is always His invitation to us.[33] Jesus is the Center of the plan. He is the Alpha or the beginning of it; He is the Omega or the end of it.[34] He is the Author and Finisher of our faith and our salvation.[35] He is in all things, through all things.[36] "All things . . . are the typifying of Him."[37] He is the Way—God's higher Way for us to return to Him.[38] There is no other Way![39] As President Russell M. Nelson taught, "Whatever questions or problems you have, the answer is always found in the life and teachings of Jesus Christ."[40] Yes, the answer is always Jesus!

The figure below shows how God's pattern with Jesus at the center moves us among the stages of faith. As we navigate to Him, we will stay on the covenant path back to God. The catalyst that initiates change from one stage to another is experiencing an opposition of

God's Pattern of Faith**

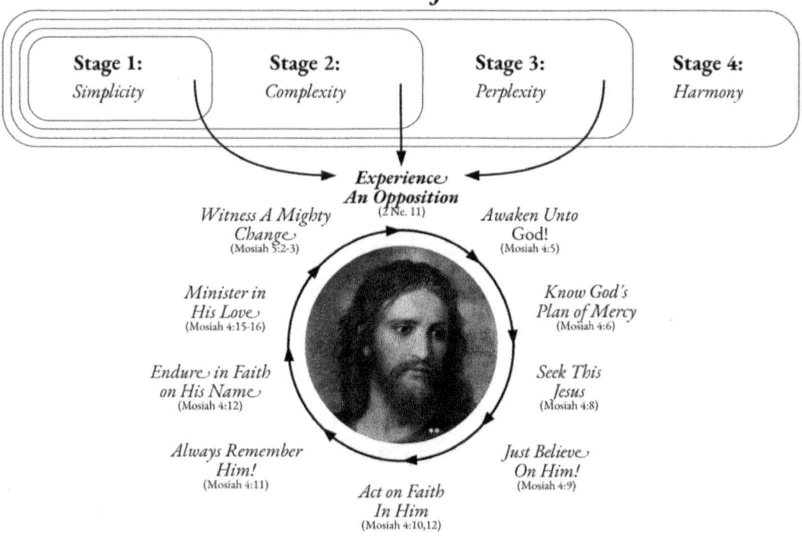

some kind. This opposition could be doubt, or it could be a different type of negative event: a loss, a rebuke, an illness, or a heartbreak. The catalyst could also be a positive event: the birth of a child, securing a job, or another unexpected blessing. When these events occur, we should follow the remainder of God's pattern if we wish to effectively navigate the change that will occur.

First, we should awaken to the gaps or needs in our lives and understand how the issue we are facing fits into God's plan of mercy. Next, we should seek Jesus, just believing on Him when our doubts peak, and acting on faith in Him even though unknowns may abound in the moment. As we always remember Him, endure in faith on His name, and minister in love to all those around us, we will experience a mighty change "in process of time."[41] That mighty change is a complete conversion to Jesus, enabling us to become more like Him.

At each stage, we must consistently navigate to Jesus through all our experiences, ensuring that He is the tie that binds all our stages together. In simplicity, we must have a basic and abiding faith in Him. In complexity, we must seek to frame any new, unsettling information considering Jesus Christ and His infinite Atonement. In perplexity, Jesus must be the iron rod—the Word of God—whom we cling to when our doubts and crises bear down upon us. When He is our foundation, we cannot fall.[42] Finally, in harmony, we must integrate our newfound understanding using our faith in Jesus Christ, or we risk embracing pleasing ideologies which reduce inner conflict but do not bring eternal life.

Navigating to Jesus moves us through our stages of faith.[43] Jesus *is* the answer to each stage of our journey of spiritual growth. Navigating to Jesus *enables* God's pattern of faith. He is the key to our progress. Jesus is also the key to our salvation because "there [is] no other name given nor any other way nor means whereby salvation can come unto the children of men, only in and through the name of Christ, the Lord Omnipotent."[44]

THE PURPOSE AND STRUCTURE OF THIS BOOK

We wrote this book to help you navigate to Jesus as you experience God's pattern of faith. By finding Him in its principles, you can more conscientiously follow Jesus and eventually become like Him as you progress along your faith journey. Jesus is the answer that will navigate you through your personal faith journey in a way that helps you remain true to Him and to His restored gospel. You will also be prepared to help others in your circle of influence to progress by connecting them to Jesus on their journey.

We are *not* saying that following this pattern will resolve every issue or answer every question you may have. Some questions and doubts may remain. Neither are we saying that faith alone can remove mental illnesses, emotional disorders, or severe trauma that legitimately require professional medical interventions and counseling.

We *are* saying that by coming unto Jesus Christ through God's pattern of faith, you will spiritually grow through life's positive and negative experiences because you will find renewed faith and confidence in Him. Jesus is and always will be enough to calm your fears and dampen your doubts. He will enable you to grow and become like your heavenly parents. His grace *is* sufficient![45]

Each chapter in this book details a principle we discovered in God's pattern of faith, which will help you navigate to Jesus on your spiritual journey. The chapters are as follows:

Chapter 1: Experience an Opposition
Chapter 2: Awaken Unto God!
Chapter 3: Know God's Plan of Mercy
Chapter 4: Seek This Jesus
Chapter 5: Just Believe on Him!
Chapter 6: Act on Faith in Him
Chapter 7: Always Remember Him!
Chapter 8: Endure in Faith on His Name
Chapter 9: Minister in His Love
Chapter 10: Witness a Mighty Change

We discuss navigating to Jesus in each element of God's pattern of faith by sharing stories from our own and others' journeys of faith. At the end of each chapter, we present questions for you to consider and space is provided for your answers. In appendix A, we provide three scriptural examples of individuals who experienced their own faith journey. In appendix B, we provide a blank template of all questions with space to write your responses where you can record your entire journey in one place. Your spiritual journey of faith is between you and God. Our book is simply a guide to assist and enable you to connect to your Savior as you progress.

Our use of the word *we* in this book is our recognition that we, as authors and you, as readers, are all on journeys of faith. The insights we share are as much for us as they are for you. As you prayerfully seek to learn the principles we share and answer the questions we present, we hope that you find yourself drawing closer to Jesus Christ as you more effectively navigate to Him on your journey of faith.

Jesus is the primary thread that binds God's pattern of faith together. He is the thread that will bind you to God via covenants. He is the Light that will guide you on your journey of faith. And He is the Way for all God's children to achieve their eternal potential. There is no other Way!

1
EXPERIENCE AN OPPOSITION

For it must needs be, that there is an opposition in all things. If not so . . . righteousness could not be brought to pass, neither wickedness, neither holiness nor misery, neither good nor bad.

—2 NEPHI 2:11

Julie: Aaron and I were high school sweethearts. We met each other while members of our school's state championship marching band. Aaron was already a member of The Church of Jesus Christ of Latter-day Saints. Although I had taken some of the missionary discussions and had attended Church meetings, I had not felt the desire to join. However, one summer everything changed.

I had gone with other youth from our ward to our stake youth conference. We heard messages from many wonderful speakers about Jesus and His gospel, and something changed in me. The messages touched my heart, and I felt the great desire to be baptized; I wanted to follow Jesus. I approached one of my young women leaders and said, "I want to get baptized. How do I do that?" She was surprised and thrilled. And to be honest, so was I. This event unexpectedly pushed me forward.

I started taking the missionary discussions more earnestly, and I let my parents know about my feelings. Soon after that, my mom brought home some anti-Church pamphlets someone at work had given her. Based on the incorrect information in those materials, she had concerns about my desire to join the Church of Jesus Christ.

One day I came home from school, and I noticed some Church-related pamphlets on the kitchen table. My stepfather had received them from a friend at work who was a member of the Church. The discussion with his friend calmed my parents' initial fears, but it didn't change their minds. They still didn't approve of my joining the Church.

I had a decision to make. Would I stop going to church and give up my desire to be baptized because I didn't have my parents' permission? I wanted to follow Jesus, so despite the opposition, I continued to attend church activities even though I couldn't be baptized. Several years later (during my freshman year of college), I turned eighteen and finally joined the Church. Aaron was away at school, and I hadn't told him about my decision to be baptized. When I called him the night of my baptism, he asked, "Why didn't you tell me?" My answer was simple: "I did this for me, not for you!"

I believe that both the spiritual jolt at that youth conference and the opposition to my baptism were necessary to prepare me to join the Church. In a miraculous way, these contrasting events moved me forward along the covenant path, not away from it. Why? The answer is Jesus.

In this chapter, we will discuss the catalyst for connecting to Jesus and moving forward on our journey of faith through experiencing "an opposition in all things." We take this phrase from 2 Nephi 2:11–12 (emphasis added):

> There is *an opposition in all things*. If not so . . . righteousness could not be brought to pass, neither wickedness, neither holiness nor misery, neither good nor bad. Wherefore, all things must needs be a compound in one; wherefore, if it should be one body it must needs remain as dead, having no life neither death, nor corruption nor incorruption, happiness nor misery, neither sense nor insensibility.

> Wherefore, [the earth] must needs have been created for a thing of naught; wherefore there would have been no purpose in the end of its creation. Wherefore, this thing must needs destroy the wisdom of God and his eternal purposes, and also the power, and the mercy, and the justice of God.

Opposition is hostility to or disagreement with something. Certainly, we experience great opposition in this life. However, the scripture above says that "*an* opposition in all things" exists. The word *an* in front of *opposition* suggests the word *opposition* in this context is more than just hostility or negativity. The phrase suggests that we will have *contrasting* experiences that could be bad or good, depending on what we choose to do with them.

For example, experiencing poor health stands in opposition or contrast to good health. Poor health can be difficult and even deadly. However, either poor *or* good health could be spiritually good or bad.

For example, if we have perennially good health but fail to express gratitude to God for this blessing, we may become prideful. We might look down on others who have poor health as being less favored of God, or we could even blame their situation on their choices. If this happens, we become less like our heavenly parents and more like the natural man or woman. Good health would then lead us away from God—not toward Him—because of our choices.

Alternatively, if we experience poor health—such as being diagnosed with a terminal condition, having a traumatic accident, or experiencing chronic mental illness—we could find greater faith in Jesus Christ as we seek His healing. We might develop deeper humility as we experience the love and support of family and friends. We may have greater empathy and compassion for others when they have poor health. We might reach out to comfort and sustain others in their trials, thus becoming more like our heavenly parents. In this example, poor health led us to God because of our choices. Therefore, good and poor health are "*an* opposition"—contrasting experiences that only become eternally good or bad based on our choice of how to handle them.

A lifetime of decisions made in the face of opposing forces both refines and reveals who we truly are. Consider how a grain of sand irritates the human eye, causing damage over time; yet in an oyster, that same irritation yields a radiant pearl. The difference lies in the inherent nature of the eye versus that of the oyster. Likewise, our divine nature as children of heavenly parents should enable us to flourish through adversity, but our choices profoundly influence the outcome.

We experience contrasts of ease and difficulty in mortality. When we understand that our lives will move on a continuum between these two types of opposition—each with its blessings and challenges—then we can find peace and forward progress as we grow. The change, or even the intensifying of each type of opposition, provides a catalyst for a new phase of eternal progress.

Without these contrasting events, we read that "all things will be a compound in one,"[46] meaning we would have no way to distinguish between good and bad, and we would not know true joy because we did not experience authentic pain. Pain can be a conduit to joy, and darkness can be a path to light. As Isaiah taught, "The people that walked in darkness have seen a great light."[47] But pain can also lead to bitterness and light to pride. Again, our choices govern the outcome.

Ultimately, hearing the doctrine and principles of the restored gospel can be the most powerful contrast needed to catalyze spiritual change. Alma discovered that "the preaching of the word had a great tendency to lead the people to do that which was just—yea, *it had more powerful effect* upon the minds of the people than the sword or anything else, which had happened to them."[48] Why? When faithless individuals hear the good news of the gospel of Jesus Christ, it contrasts with their current life of sin or faithlessness. The Spirit accompanies the teaching of the gospel, and He can open their eyes to its beauty and importance and help them to see what they have been missing. Many converts to the restored Church begin their journey of conversion in this way—by listening and responding to a simple message about Jesus Christ given by humble missionaries.

The opposing experiences described above catalyze our next stage of faith, as shown in the figure in the preface of this book. When we are comfortable in the simplicity stage, encountering complexity initiates a new phase of growth. This complexity is an opposition.

When we deal with complexity, we may face a significant crisis—a strong opposing force that pushes us into perplexity. And when we have wrestled sufficiently long and well in perplexity, our new or strengthened faith is a contrasting experience that impels us forward into harmony. Opposition initiates change. And change is necessary for our eternal progression.

Some individuals experience greater periods of opposition than others. Like the differences recounted in the parable of the talents,[49] some people are given a greater number or variety of contrasting experiences than others. What we do with those experiences matters more than their number or type. Those who grow proportionally to the opposition they are given will be told, "Well done, thou good and faithful servant."[50] If we don't capitalize on these experiences,[51] we could find ourselves spiritually anemic from our lack of spiritual growth.

The growth of a seed is an instructive analogy from nature for the role of an opposition in our spiritual growth. Seeds must overcome the force of gravity and the weight of the dirt above them to grow. They must push their shoots through the earth—upward toward the sun and downward toward nutrients and water. We've often wondered how seeds distinguish *up* from *down* and how they know which way to send their shoots and which way to send their roots. We learned that physical phenomena called *gravitropism* and *phototropism* govern a seed's growth.[52]

Gravitropism is the growth movement of a plant in response to gravity.[53] The roots respond *positively* to gravity, meaning they grow *toward* its pull, while the shoots respond *negatively*, meaning they grow *away* from its downward force. Gravity is the same for roots and shoots, but how they respond to that powerful force is very different.

Plants "perceive" gravity using particles called statoliths in their cells. These particles contain organelles that are heavier than the gel-like substance within the cell membrane. The organelles settle to the bottom of the cell due to gravity, which triggers hormones in that part of the cell. This concentration of hormones at the bottom of plant cells is a signal that tells the seed which way roots and shoots should grow.

Once the first shoots come out of the ground, phototropism begins to take effect. Phototropism is the upward response of a plant to a light stimulus. The plant grows upward toward the light and away from the gravity-concentrated hormones at the bottom of the plant's cells. The oppositional process associated with gravitropism and phototropism is a defined opposition that leads to a healthy plant whose roots reach downward into the earth and whose stems and leaves reach upward toward the sun.[54]

Likewise, we must face an opposition as we spiritually grow, working against the "gravity" of our imperfect mortal life to grow spiritually. To accomplish this growth, we must tap into the sources of spiritual power from above, like revelation from the Holy Ghost, and nutrition from below, like the scriptures, our patriarchal blessings, or living prophets. Doing so will enable us to learn from all the contrasting experiences of mortality, which can catalyze and enable our spiritual growth.

The verses in 2 Nephi 2:11–12 identify five concepts associated with an opposition: It must needs be, It provides purpose for God's creation, It protects the wisdom of God, It enables His power, and It unlocks His mercy and justice. We will discuss each in detail to clarify the role of an opposition on our journey of faith in Jesus.

IT MUST NEEDS BE

The first important concept related to an opposition is that "it must needs be,"[55] meaning we can't avoid it. It just is. Despite its pervasiveness and our recognition that it can't be avoided, we often experience deep and sometimes troubling questions regarding the opposition we witness or experience.

Why is life hard for some but easy for others? Why do some suffer immensely while others never seem to suffer? Why do evil people prosper and the righteous fail? Why is our joy sweet yet fleeting while sorrows seem to linger? Do these things have to be? These questions may be among the most difficult to answer in this life. We do not claim to know all the reasons, but we believe that understanding the universality of an opposition can help frame the questions properly.

All people are intimately familiar with contrasts in this life. Up and down, left and right, light and darkness, health and sickness, pleasure and pain—the list is infinite. "An opposition" must needs be. Perhaps the Lord was teaching us an eternal principle in that statement: An opposition exists, and we can't escape it.

Intuitively, we know that opposition can make us better and help us progress. No athlete becomes a champion without facing an opponent. Champions only emerge when they overcome opponents and win. Yet when contrasting experiences come, we can forget their purpose and often question why they are happening.

Instead of trying to explain "an opposition," perhaps we should just accept that contrasts are part of "things as they really are, and of things as they really will be."[56] Our acceptance isn't ambivalence or pessimism; it's a recognition of a fundamental truth. By embracing contrasts as a permanent and purposeful part of our existence, we are better able to choose what to do with them. Our highest and best choice is to have them draw us to the Savior, who will succor, sustain, and save us. Elder Neal A Maxwell taught this need to focus on Christ in our contrasting experiences:

> We should, therefore brothers and sisters, see life as being comprised of clusters of soul-stretching experiences. Even when these are overlain by seeming ordinariness or are wrapped in routine.
>
> There is clearly no immunity from these stimuli. There cannot be. No immunity from afflictions. There cannot be. Whether the afflictions are self-induced, as most of them are, or are of the divine tutorial type, it matters not. Either way, the Lord can help us in a most interesting manner. Our afflictions, said Alma, can be 'swallowed up in the joy of Christ' (Alma 31:38). Thus, afflictions are endured and are overcome by being overwhelmed by joy as the sour notes are lost amid a symphony of salvational sounds. Our afflictions, brothers and sisters, often will not be extinguished; they will be dwarfed and swallowed up in the joy of Christ. That's how we overcome most of the time—it's not their elimination, but the placing of them in that larger context [of Christ].[57]

Opposition enables us to better understand the world around us and God above us. Most importantly, it exists to give us purpose, power, and ultimately, redemption through Christ.

PROVIDES PURPOSE FOR THE EARTH'S CREATION

The second important concept related to an opposition is that it provides purpose for earth's creation.[58] We were created to become like our heavenly parents, and we can only arrive at this destination if we choose wisely while experiencing mortality.[59] "To bring about [God's] eternal purposes . . . it must needs be that there was an opposition. . . . Wherefore, [people] could not act for [themselves] save it should be that [they were] enticed by the one or the other."[60] God designed this mortal world to be the place for His children to experience this enticement of contrasting options.

During this life we face myriad contrasts. We witness births and deaths. We see justice served and injustices abound. We observe the beauty of nature and the ugliness of pollution. We watch service and sacrifice lift the downtrodden, and we watch the rich and powerful "grind the faces of the poor."[61] These contrasts are the very purpose of the world's creation. Here, we are to experience mortality and a limited life so we can eventually enjoy immortality and eternal life.

President Spencer W. Kimball taught the principle that mortality's contrasts facilitate our eternal development.

> Is there not wisdom in [God] giving us trials that we might rise above them [in mortality], responsibilities that we might achieve, work to harden our muscles, sorrows to try our souls? Are we not exposed to temptations to test our strength, sickness that we might learn patience, death that we might be immortalized and glorified?
>
> If all the sick for whom we pray were healed, if all the righteous were protected and the wicked destroyed, the whole program of the Father would be annulled and the basic principle of the gospel, free agency, would be ended. No man [or woman] would have to live by faith.[62]

Without faith in the Lord Jesus Christ, we would never be able to overcome opposition and return to the presence of God.

Absent life's opposing experiences—persecution and peace or sorrow and elation—the Saints could never build the Christlike character that enables them to become like God, which is His business and our life's purpose. As Elder Neal A. Maxwell once observed, "If one were to press me to say, 'What does being about our Father's business consist of, in summational terms,' I would say being about our Father's business is to be about the business of becoming like His Only Begotten Son, Jesus Christ."[63] Through opposition, the faithful progress, and the wicked regress.

Without an opposition, God's plan and purpose would be frustrated because mortal life would have no meaning. We would have no righteousness or happiness because we would not have experienced wickedness or misery. "All things must have vanished away."[64] With opposition, disciples of Christ will have the opportunity to traverse the "strait and narrow course" of life and land "at the right hand of God" through their faith in the Savior.[65]

PROTECTS THE WISDOM OF GOD

The third important concept related to an opposition is that it protects the wisdom of God.[66] Wisdom is "the quality of having experience, knowledge and good judgment."[67] The wisdom of God is perfect and eternal. Using His perfect judgment, He accomplishes His purpose to perfect His children while respecting their agency and simultaneously working within the circumstances of mortality.

God must know when and how to intervene and when to allow events to play out. And He must do this for millions of His children simultaneously, when each desires blessings that must be sequenced properly with the desires of others to achieve the most good for the most people. The Lord's comment that all things must be done "in wisdom and in order" is not just counsel for us, it is also a divine commentary on His approach to caring for the many needs and circumstances of His children.[68] He must use His wisdom to sequence and deliver His divine design, or else He could violate agency and "cease to be God."[69]

Despite God's infinite wisdom in accomplishing so much good for so many people, we often question His methods and His motives. Why would He allow suffering to occur at all or for an extended time for one person or an entire people? Why might one person receive a significant unexpected blessing while someone seemingly more deserving may not?

Once again, we do not have the answers to such important questions. However, an opposition allows God to do His perfect work for His children in wisdom and in order. If God were not allowed to use contrasts in dealing with His children, His wisdom would be compromised and, ultimately destroyed, as Lehi taught.[70]

Imagine if God could only give positive blessings to all His children all the time and if all pain, suffering, and loss were prevented by Him. How would humility and meekness be developed in a world where everyone received everything they always wanted? How would patience be produced if no one ever had to wait? How would courage be cultivated if no dangers existed? How would faith in the Lord Jesus Christ be fostered if we always knew exactly the next step we should take in our lives? How could obedience be observed if there were no commandments? Surely these situations would lead to spiritually weak Saints and prideful children of God. God's wisdom would be compromised, as would His purpose in helping His children become more like Him.

Without an opposition, God could not wisely manage us through our stages of faith. We might remain stuck in any one stage because we would experience no catalytic event to trigger our need for change. As Elder Boyd K. Packer wisely observed, "Things that don't change stay the same . . . and when we are through changing—*we're through*."[71] However, by accessing an opposition, God can make sure that change happens just as He ensures that "all things work together for good to them that love God, to them who are the called according to his purpose."[72]

God's wise use of opposition is not easy. Change is hard. Opposition is hard. Paul wisely taught, "Now no chastening *for the present* seemeth to be joyous, but grievous: nevertheless *afterward* it yieldeth the peaceable fruit of righteousness unto them which are exercised thereby."[73]

We don't often like it when challenging things occur in our lives. However, afterward we can see the "peaceable fruits" to which Paul refers: patience, long-suffering, gentleness, and charity. These character traits—along with myriad other blessings—often come precisely because of an opposition in our lives. The faith and patience we develop after the process is complete will far outweigh the grievousness we feel during it. In time, we will see and appreciate God's wisdom in the order of His using an opposition for our experience and good.[74]

Aaron: In 2019, I was released as bishop. During this emotional time of change, I was feeling the loss of serving in such an intimate and intense calling that had allowed me to feel God's love for His children in unique ways. It was difficult. Then the other shoe dropped. I was notified that because of cost-cutting measures, my job—along with the jobs of several other senior executives at our health system—was unexpectedly cut; we were all left to find new jobs.

I was shocked and devastated. I had just served for nearly six years over two different wards as bishop. Thoughts such as, "Why would this happen to me when I had served so faithfully?" and "Why wasn't I protected from this event?" came to my mind.

Of course, bad things can happen to good people. But this fact did not numb the pain of being released as bishop, compounded by the sting of my job loss.

Shortly after I began my job search, I received a huge tender mercy. A recruiter reached out to me about a senior partner role in a healthcare consulting firm. I had been a consultant after business school, so I was comfortable with that kind of role. As I learned more about the firm, I began to feel a sense of peace that this was the job for me. Despite an expected increase in travel that I wouldn't prefer, I felt that I should take the job. My father gave me a blessing that confirmed this, so I moved forward and accepted the position.

Despite the initial difficulty and pain, the experience of losing my job and finding a new one was a significant blessing. I found my new position so quickly that we were able to use much of my severance pay to get out of debt. We had been praying to find a way to be debt-free for several years, but we would never have imagined that this blessing would come by losing a job.

In 2020, just six months after I started my new job, the whole world shut down due to the COVID-19 pandemic. Instead of traveling frequently as I had feared, I ended up working from home. If I had remained a senior executive in a health system during COVID, I would have worked more hours, not fewer. In addition, those nearly two years of not traveling allowed me to spend a great deal of time with my father, who died unexpectedly in April 2021. That period also gave Julie and me ample free time to write our first book—something which we never had anticipated.[75]

I cannot deny the pain I felt in losing my job. However, I can also not deny the blessings that came out of that pain. God's way *is* higher than our way. His wisdom was far greater than ours. In this case, His wisdom in allowing us to experience the contrasts of losing and finding a job gave us precious blessings we would not have had otherwise. We never would have willingly chosen this path, but we will be forever grateful for the experience it provided.

ENABLES THE POWER OF GOD

The fourth important concept related to an opposition is that it enables the power of God. Power is defined as "the ability or capacity to do something . . . to direct or influence the behavior of others or the course of events . . . [the] strength and force exerted by something or someone.[76] God's power, therefore, is His ability or capacity to carry out His purpose "to bring to pass the immortality and eternal life of [His children]."[77] His power is priesthood power. God also harnesses the power of faith to accomplish His work.[78] If His sole purpose is focused on us, then His power, too, must be wholly concentrated on *our* progression, not on *His* pleasure.

God taught us that His honor is His power.[79] Honor is trust. God can receive perfect trust from us because of His perfect nature. He is perfectly loving, kind, patient, and gentle. He teaches and corrects perfectly. Because He has no flaws, loves perfectly, and does all things for the benefit of others, all of His creations can have perfect confidence in Him. Therefore, He has perfect power through His perfect honor.

With His perfect power, God can do all things, including heal, comfort, and redeem us.[80] However, He will not use His power to force us to change or compel us to seek His healing and guidance. He acts by persuasion—not by compulsion—always exhibiting long-suffering, gentleness, meekness, and love unfeigned.[81]

Ultimately, Jesus Christ, God's Beloved Son, is the embodiment and Conveyor of God's power.[82] Through His Son, who completed a "perfect atonement, wrought by the shedding of [His] blood,"[83] God the Father can redeem all His children who willingly choose Him.

So how does an opposition enable His power? Jesus can only use His power on our behalf if we allow it. We must *choose* His help; we must *choose* to change. Choice can only exist when multiple options are presented, and an opposition provides those options. Contrasts catalyze choices, and choices enable agency.

Moral agency, which is protected by God, is our most important eternal gift. Why? Only through our agency can we freely and willingly continue our spiritual development without outside compulsion. There is no other way. Agency is the key to accessing the blessings Jesus Christ can provide through His infinite and eternal Atonement.

Choice causes change, and positive change can lead to spiritual growth. Easy choices lead to slow change, and hard choices persuade us to change faster. Good choices lead to positive change; poor choices lead to negative change. Choice, consequence, and change are inseparably connected, and we learn in these moments.

For example, the Lord commands us to pray, but the adversary teaches us not to pray.[84] This opposition creates a choice: We can choose to pray or not. When we choose to pray, the promised blessings and power from God freely flow to us, and He accomplishes His purpose. Opposition unlocks His ability to guide and send spiritual power to us when we pray.

Likewise, we understand that "in the ordinances [and their associated covenants], the power of God is manifest."[85] God offers us covenants, but the world tells us we have no need of covenants. When we choose to willingly make and keep these sacred promises and forge a new relationship with God, we will observe meaningful changes in our spiritual lives—slowly but surely. We will experience growth and receive spiritual gifts, which give us a small portion of His power and capabilities. And if we continue becoming like Him by living our covenants, we will use these special gifts to help others on their journey of eternal progression. In this way, His power *in* us and *through* us will be obvious.

These simple examples of prayer and covenants can extend to every other gospel doctrine or principle. His power to heal, guide, and redeem us through His Son is facilitated by an opposition. Through our humble, submissive choices, we can progress spiritually because we willingly access God's priesthood power.

In contrast, the scriptures describe individuals who are not progressing spiritually as having a hard heart. A person with a hard heart is one who is not meek and humble, who resists the promptings of the Spirit, and who remains grounded in biases and false ideas of right and wrong. God's power is *not* manifest in them because they reject it.

One type of hard-hearted person hears the voice of God but does not respond by following Him. Another type allows trials to cause them to become bitter and resentful, leading them away from God, not toward Him. The Nephites in the Book of Mormon experienced a period when due to the great length of a war, some were "hardened," but many others "were softened because of their afflictions."[86] Contrasting choices led to contrasting outcomes.

Another type of hard-hearted person is so assertive about the truth and the commandments that they try coercing others into obedience or condemning others for their imperfections instead of loving them. They may become judgmental, wondering (like the brother of the prodigal son) why others can't "get with the program," or worse, hoping they "get what they deserve."[87] This person may impose the first great commandment upon their neighbor instead of living the second great commandment, which is to love our neighbor by finding a way to gently persuade and to forgive when repentance is sought.

These individuals may be stuck in the simplicity stage where their faith has become a narrowly understood universal rule without a broader understanding or experience. Without catalytic change, they can become dogmatic, accusing those who are truly seeking the truth of being unfaithful or seeking harsh judgments even when sincere repentance is pursued. They misunderstand that the Savior's admonition to "seek and ye shall find" is meant to be the effort of a lifetime.[88] Finding the restored truth doesn't mean a person should stop spiritually seeking. On the contrary, perhaps their initial discovery means that the journey of seeking has just begun, and future inquiry is necessary to embrace the paradoxes of life which those truths will eventually uncover.

Softening a hard heart requires some kind of force—an opposition in all things—which catalyzes change. This energy must overcome the stationary position of someone who has a stagnant faith. In physics, an object at rest has potential energy, but an active outside force is needed to overcome friction and move it. Similarly, an outside opposition will generate and sustain our inner change. And positive change accomplishes God's purpose and demonstrates His power.

Julie: Shortly after I was baptized, I was called into my bishop's office and called as the Primary teacher for the oldest class of girls. I was so nervous about this calling. As a new convert, I knew very little about our doctrine, and I didn't know any of the Primary songs. The bishop assured me that Heavenly Father wanted me to serve, so I accepted.

At first, my calling was difficult. I had to study the lessons in the Primary manual to teach my class, and much of the information was new to me. I also had to learn the Primary songs. Everything in Primary was new to me. My learning curve was steep, but I moved forward with faith in my Savior.

Despite my initial challenges, this calling became precious to me. I learned the gospel along with my Primary girls. I had them over to my house for activities. They were sweet, and I came to love them. I felt closer to my Savior than I had felt before as I served the best I could.

One Sunday, I slept in later than usual because we didn't have our regular Sunday meeting schedule. My mom came in to wake me up, concerned that I would be late for church. I told her about the time change, and she apologized for disturbing me. I realized at that moment that the difficulties of my calling had changed not only me, but they had also changed my parents. Their concerns with the Church had turned to an interest in helping me serve. God's power was evident in the difficulties and opportunities of that little Primary calling.

UNLOCKS HIS MERCY AND JUSTICE

The final outcome of an opposition is that it unlocks God's mercy and justice. Mercy is the suspension of a deserved punishment. As we pursue a course of change and strive to accomplish God's will for us, we will make mistakes, and we will sin. Imperfections are inevitable in mortality. Only One ever lived perfectly: Jesus Christ. Everyone else needs redemption from their sins and mistakes. Fortunately, that One sacrificed Himself for us, so He could offer us mercy and redemption through His infinite and eternal Atonement. He is the only Way.

Mercy would not be needed if sin and mistakes were not made. And without missteps we would never reach our full potential. In a paradoxical way, mistakes lead to perfection—but only through the merits and mercy of Jesus Christ. Therefore, the opposition that fulfilled God's purpose also necessitated a Savior, unlocking the Redeemer's perfect mercy and perfect justice.

Contrasts can also invite us to have mercy and love for others. At some point, another person will offend, abuse, or harm us—either incidentally or purposely. That hurt requires us to heal, and part of the healing process includes extending mercy and forgiveness to the offender. "I, the Lord, will forgive whom I will forgive, but of *you* it is required to forgive all [people]."[89] Mercy extended to others will return to us in the form of peace and love. Therefore, an opposition gives us the opportunity to learn how to be more like Jesus Christ as we, in turn, offer mercy to others.

An opposition also enables God's perfect justice. We may see justice as simply being the opposite of mercy. Because mercy suspends just punishments, we might view justice as delivering merited punishments. However, God will be justified in extending the maximum mercy that a person can merit "because of his loving kindness and his long-suffering towards the children of men."[90] We may be surprised at how much mercy *we* receive in the final judgment, so we should not be surprised when we see such abundant mercy offered to *others*—even to those who have offended or harmed us.

Elder J. Ruben Clark beautifully stated, "I believe that his juridical concept of his dealings with his children could be expressed in this way: I believe that in his justice and mercy he will give us the maximum reward for our acts, give us all that he can give, and in the reverse, I believe that he will impose upon us the minimum penalty which it is possible for him to impose."[91] We will be witnesses of that abundant gift of Christ's mercy, and we will exclaim, "Great and marvelous are thy works; . . . just and true are thy ways!"[92]

Indeed, an opposition unleashes God's mercy and justice. Jesus experienced our opposition Himself. Why? "That his bowels may be filled with mercy, according to the flesh, that he may know according to the flesh how to succor his people according to their infirmities."[93] What love and perfect comprehension by our perfect Savior and Redeemer!

May we call on Jesus to use His perfect understanding to assist us in our contrasting experiences. As we do, our positive progress along our journey of faith will increase as will our faith and trust in Him.

QUESTIONS TO CONSIDER

1. What type of opposition (difficulty or ease) are you currently facing? How is difficulty an opposition for you? Why? How is ease an opposition for you? Why?
2. In what ways is that opposition a barrier to your progress? Why? In what ways is that opposition a catalyst for your progress? Why?
3. How have contrasting experiences in your life enabled the Lord's mercy for you?
4. How have you seen Jesus in your opposition? How has that realization helped you progress?
5. How can you find joy in your opposition? How could those feelings sustain you in your most difficult times?

NOTES AND INSIGHTS

2

AWAKEN UNTO GOD!

Awake, awake, put on thy strength,
O Zion; put on thy beautiful garments. . . .
Shake thyself from the dust; arise and sit down.

—ISAIAH 52:1

Aaron: Everyone has gifts and talents. Growing up, I realized that one of my talents was in academics. I loved learning, so I always loved school. I never found going to school to be a chore. I was excited by my classes. Grades were never an issue for me because they were just the natural outcome of the learning process I enjoyed.

My family was of modest means, and my parents made it very clear that in order to go to college, I would need to get a scholarship. Given that my talents were in academics, I set the goal to receive an academic scholarship to attend Brigham Young University.

Our high school operated on a one-hundred-point grading system. To achieve the highest class ranking, I would need to score near one hundred on my assignments. In every class, I became obsessed with getting the highest grades. Getting an A wasn't enough; I had to score perfectly on everything. Julie remembers a time when I got a 99 on an assignment, and I was livid. Looking back, this behavior seems so foolish, but at the time my grades were my top priority.

To make things worse, in my quest for perfect grades, I saw my classmates as opponents. I pitted myself against them in every class and on every assignment. I also tried to be in as many leadership positions as possible because I knew it would increase my chances to receive a scholarship. This required me to win leadership elections.

I thrived in this hyper-competitive academic environment. I finished high school ranked third in my class, and I was elected president of the honor society and president of our state champion marching band. In the fall of my senior year, I applied to BYU and received a full-ride four-year scholarship. I had achieved my goal! All was well—or so I thought.

In the spring of my senior year of high school (April 1989), I was watching general conference and heard a talk that hit me like a lightning bolt. The talk, "Beware of Pride,"[94] was from President Ezra Taft Benson but was delivered by President Gordon B. Hinckley due to President Benson's poor health.

In his masterful discourse, President Benson detailed the universal sin of pride. He said that the core of pride was enmity—hostility or opposition to God and to others. Listening to this talk, I realized that I had been a most prideful student. Academically, I had pitted myself against everyone and thought I was better than anyone. At that moment, I had an awakening to my terrible, prideful condition. I realized that I needed to change.

In the intervening years, I have had other academic experiences (including undergraduate and graduate degrees), and I have achieved similar academic success. However, I tried to work *with* my fellow students and not *against* them. I came to see our learning time as a joint experience instead of a competitive one. I began to value the talents and perspectives of others. I shared my notes and ideas with my classmates to help them succeed. I studied with others on teams. As a result, my overall educational experience was much richer, as were my relationships with my classmates.

I am by no means perfectly humble. I still struggle with the universal sin of pride, but I work to eliminate it from my life. However, this awakening during my senior year of high school brought to my attention one of my major deficiencies, and this awareness has made a great difference in my life.

In this chapter, we will discuss the process of awakening unto God. Alma the Younger, in describing the outcome of his father's work among the people of Limhi, said that God "changed their hearts; yea, he awakened them out of a deep sleep, and *they awoke unto God*. Behold, they were in the midst of darkness; nevertheless, their souls were illuminated by the light of the everlasting word."[95] When they "awakened unto God" they were "illuminated by the light of the everlasting word." Who is that Word? The Word is Jesus Christ, who always points us back to His Father and who strengthens and enables our journey of faith.[96]

What does it mean to "awaken unto God"? To awaken to Him is to become clearly aware of God's influence in our lives. We must also become aware of His Beloved Son, for the Father always points us to Him. We can come to understand Jesus's great role in the plan of salvation, which is to be our Redeemer, Advocate, and Judge. Anytime we receive a blessing or intervention from God, we must understand that Jesus is at the helm, directing those efforts on our behalf.

A sister once told us, "I pray to Heavenly Father, and I know He hears and answers my prayers, but I'm not sure exactly how the Savior fits into the picture. I feel close to my Heavenly Father, but not to my Savior." Our response to this sweet seeking sister was, "Every answer you've received and every comforting feeling you've had when you pray to the Father has come through Jesus. Jesus directs and interfaces with you on behalf of the Father through the Holy Spirit who is the conduit of that communication." She smiled as she realized that those tender feelings she had for her loving Heavenly Father were also feelings she had for her Savior because He was the one from whom she received the Father's answers. This sister had a wonderful awakening.

Spiritual awakening includes becoming aware of our own spiritual strengths and weaknesses. Awakening also means becoming cognizant of the strengths and weaknesses of others, noticing opportunities to work with and learn from them or to uplift and edify them. Awakening unto God is the beginning of the process of conversion or growth, which culminates when we eventually receive a "mighty change . . . in our hearts"[97] and turn to the Lord "with full purpose of heart."[98]

How does our illumination begin? We would suggest that the opposition we discussed in the last chapter is our catalyst to the process of awakening. It shakes us from our spiritual sleep and opens our eyes to new realities—a sometimes difficult process depending on the depth of our personal unawareness or the extent of our spiritual naiveté. An opposition creates difficulty and sometimes desperation. In that condition, we seek answers and meaning. We should seek Jesus.

At first, we may seek for meaning in the circumstance itself—a logical starting point. Struggling with perplexing issues, we may look outward to understand the cause of the issue we are facing. Instead of framing the issue with our faith in Jesus, we can mistakenly frame our faith with the issue we face. This reversed framing can lead us to blame others or even God for our circumstances in that search. We may falsely believe that our faith in Jesus should have prevented this hard thing from happening; we may even fault our faith, or lack of it.

In some cases, our circumstances may have been caused by something or someone else. However, peace can never come when we obsess over things we *cannot* control or seek to cast blame on anything or anyone. To progress, this outward focus should eventually give way to an internal evaluation of things we *can* control. This change is part of the awakening we need in order to move forward.

When we are compelled by circumstance to be humble,[99] God can begin His work with us. He will help us move forward, even while we are unaware of His intervention. As we said earlier, His way is higher than our way, and His way will always involve His beloved Son and our eternal progress.[100] His sole purpose is to help us become like Him. Why? So, we can turn and lift others of His children and help them progress as we become His agents in mortality and beyond. And this purpose can only be achieved when His children come to His only Beloved Son and "become perfected in Him."[101]

The Holy Spirit will prompt us to look inward to find those things that require change in ourselves and to look toward Jesus, whose purpose is to help and heal us. Jesus always invited His disciples to focus on their actions when facing difficulty. In His brilliant Sermon on the Mount, He told them to agree with their enemy quickly, [102] turn the other cheek when smitten,[103] love, bless, and pray for their enemies and those that hate and curse them,[104] judge not to avoid being judged,[105] look at the beam (large pole) in their eyes and not the mote (small stick) in other people's eye, and [106] do to others as they would have others do to them. [107]

Notice that each of these invitations by Jesus concentrates on the actions of the person *receiving* harm, not on the actions of the person *delivering* the harm. Jesus did not tell His disciples to fix, blame, accuse, or berate the other person. He asked them to take the higher road of love, faith, and forgiveness. Therefore, if we find something that causes us to doubt or question, perhaps we can begin to resolve the issue by focusing on our faith first and then turn outward to understand the issue at hand.

We are not suggesting that Jesus taught that people delivering harm are justified in their actions. Jesus did not *justify* the damaging actions of others. Neither did He tell His disciples to put themselves into harmful situations or to continue receiving hatred, deception, or abuse from others. He simply taught that His disciples should ensure that they strive to live a higher law *despite* others' actions. To be clear, the person receiving the harm is not the problem; the person delivering the harm is the problem. However, the person receiving the harm can be part of the solution by choosing to live Jesus's higher law of faith, hope, and charity.

The Savior's invitations also imply that we are meant to become comfortable with discomfort. Resolutions to tough situations—ones that create harm, doubt, or distress—may not come immediately or at all. However, if we awaken to God and are grounded in Christ, we can move forward anyway.

Indeed, wise disciples of Jesus look to Him to help them find meaning, strength, and comfort, whereas others look for other sources of help and support. When He is our focus, our search for meaning and help eventually leads us to our own eternal potential—to the person whom God wants us to become—and to Christ, who makes it all possible.

When we engage in this awakening process with Jesus as our guide, we will (1) become illuminated by the light of the everlasting Word, (2) recognize our current weaknesses, (3) understand our mortal identity and eternal potential, (4) see our spiritual gifts, (5) acknowledge the goodness of God, and (6) identify our compensatory blessings. We will discuss each of these actions in this chapter.

BECOMING ILLUMINATED BY THE LIGHT OF THE EVERLASTING WORD

Awakening unto God happens only when we are "illuminated by the light of the everlasting word."[108] The ancient Apostle John the Beloved taught us that Jesus Christ is the Word. He is the "light that shineth in the darkness; and the darkness comprehendeth it not."[109] "[He] is light, and in him is no darkness at all."[110] Jesus likewise taught, "I am the light of the world: he that followeth me shall not walk in darkness, but shall have the light of life."[111]

The scriptures equate light to love.[112] The light we feel when the Savior illuminates us is His pure love. God's love is the reason He sent His Beloved Son to die for us.[113] Anyone who has tasted the sweet redemption that comes through the Atonement of Jesus Christ has felt that love and light. As Nephi exclaimed, "But behold, the Lord hath redeemed my soul from hell; I have beheld his *glory* [or light], and I am encircled about eternally in the arms of his *love*."[114] As King Solomon declared, "Truly the light is sweet."[115] His love *is* sweet!

Because Jesus is the source of all light and truth, we can only awaken when He is involved. Through the light or love of Christ—that spark of divinity every child of God receives in mortality—He leads everyone to do that which is good, decent, and honorable. He leads all to become better.

As His covenant disciples, we have the added influence of the Holy Ghost. Through the Holy Ghost, Jesus Christ further enlightens our minds and gives us "great views"[116] of ourselves, our lives, and our potential. He also provides additional comfort, strength, and guidance when the opposition of mortal life catalyzes our change.[117] That intimate influence is evidence of His love.

The everlasting word to which John refers[118] is also the pure truth that comes from Jesus Christ and is found in His restored gospel. "For the word of the Lord is *truth*, and whatsoever is truth is light, and whatsoever is light is Spirit, even the Spirit of Jesus Christ."[119] What is truth? "Truth is knowledge of things [or people] as they are, and as they were, and as they are to come."[120]

Because God perfectly loves us, He wants us to understand ourselves—as we *really* were, *really* are, and *really* will be—via His Holy Spirit.[121] The process of understanding ourselves as we "really are" and of our situation as it "really is" can be jarring. We may not fully recognize what needs to change in our lives, which keeps us from successfully navigating the opposition that confronts us.

Egos are fragile, and we can feel shattered when we finally see what needs to change in ourselves. However, if we are humble and know that God has shown us this reality because He loves us and wants us to progress, then we can move forward positively and not become stuck in the mire of shame or self-pity. When we receive God's initial rays of light, that light will slowly grow within us and gently and lovingly illuminate where change is needed. "That which is of God is *love*; and he that receiveth *love*, and continueth in God, receiveth more *love*; and that *love* groweth brighter and brighter until the perfect day."[122] How beautiful!

May we always allow Jesus's light and His infinite love to prepare the way for us to grow and progress spiritually. Our awakening begins with His light—His love—and moves us forward on His path of becoming.

RECOGNIZING OUR WEAKNESS

King Benjamin explicitly states that our awakening will cause us to be more aware of our weakness—our "nothingness, and [our] worthless and fallen state"[123] when compared to the perfection of Jesus. This realization can be hard on us, but it is a necessary step to our progress. Why do we have weaknesses?

We are taught in the scriptures that Heavenly Father designed mortality to be a time of testing for His children.[124] As part of this testing, each person faces weaknesses that come to us "because of the flesh"[125] and because of the fallen world into which we are born. Weaknesses can be inherited because of genetics. Weaknesses can also be learned because of environmental or social influences. These "thorns in the flesh"[126] are different for each person. Some weaknesses are relatively minor from a spiritual standpoint.[127] Others are more spiritually serious.

Our weaknesses can lead us to make mistakes. Mistakes are not sins, but they can hurt us.[128] For example, stepping into the street in the path of an oncoming car because we are not paying attention is a mistake. However, this mistake can have serious consequences, including the loss of our lives.

Weaknesses can also lead us into temptation and sin. The adversary knows our weaknesses as well as he knows our strengths. He will do all he can to leverage those weaknesses against us, strategically placing temptations in our pathway that are targeted at our faults and flaws. If we succumb to these temptations and violate any of the laws of God, we have committed a sin, for which we must repent and be made clean.

Weaknesses are not predestination; we can and should try to overcome them by not allowing them to negatively affect us. In writing about the weakness of alcoholism, one author observed, "A high percentage of individuals with AUD [alcohol use disorder] have a genetic predisposition to the disease, although genetic predisposition can be overcome. *Genetics are risk factors, not destiny.*"[129] This same principle holds true for any of our weaknesses: they are risk factors for us and not our destiny.

Weaknesses should point us to Jesus Christ because we can be assured that through Him and His infinite Atonement, our weaknesses can become strengths.[130] In some cases, Jesus will correct our weaknesses which will be strengthened and eventually disappear. Other times, our weaknesses may not necessarily go away, however, their impact can be mitigated by Him. For example, He may inspire us with ways to protect ourselves from our faults and their attendant temptations. Or, the Lord may use our weaknesses to build His kingdom and minister to His children, effectively nullifying their negative effect and making them work for our good and His work's benefit.

Ultimately, our hope is secure when we realize that Jesus Christ already conquered all our weaknesses, so He can help us with a strategy to gain victory over them. Wise priesthood leaders, loving family members, and caring friends are all sources of succor and strength which the Savior can use in this effort.

UNDERSTANDING OUR MORTAL IDENTITY AND ETERNAL POTENTIAL

As we awaken, Jesus Christ will show us the reality of our mortal identity and our eternal potential through the Holy Ghost. Knowing who we are in this life and who we can become in the next provides purpose and power. This realization is of utmost importance because it can guide our choices—especially those choices related to our progress as we move among the stages of faith.

Each person fills multiple roles in mortality. For example, women can simultaneously act as daughters, sisters, mothers, bosses, employees, neighbors, volunteers, leaders, and a host of other roles depending on their circumstances. Men have similar opportunities. To help us prioritize these multiple roles, President Russell M. Nelson spoke of our most important mortal identities when he said, "I believe that if the Lord were speaking to you directly . . . the first thing He would make sure you understand is your true identity. . . . "*Who are you?*" First and foremost, you are a child of God. Second, as a member of the Church, you are a child of the covenant [and of the house of Israel]. And third, you are a disciple of Jesus Christ."[131]

Awakening to these three most important identities is a light to our journey through mortality.[132] This light will be discernible in the lives and countenances of the Saints of God and followers of Jesus Christ.[133] It becomes an "armour of light"[134] that keeps us on our journey to Jesus and protects us from long-term spiritual damage as we encounter difficulties on our way.

SEEING OUR SPIRITUAL GIFTS

According to the Church website, "Spiritual gifts are blessings or abilities given by God to His children through the power of the Holy Ghost. Gifts of the Spirit are given to bless and benefit those who love the Lord and seek to keep His commandments."[135] On our journey of faith, we should strive to awaken to these gifts so we can more readily access their blessings for ourselves and others. They will point us to Jesus because as His disciples, the gifts are given to us to light the world around us.

In the scriptures we are taught, "There are many [spiritual] gifts, and to every [person] is given a gift by the Spirit of God."[136] Every member of the Church is entitled to receive a gift of the Spirit. They are given so we can accomplish God's "work and glory to bring to pass the immortality and eternal life of [all]."[137] Whatever the task, our natural abilities are augmented by God's spiritual gifts.

As we endeavor to find Jesus on our journey of faith, we should awaken to our spiritual gifts because they will connect us to Him. For example, the gift of faith in the Lord Jesus Christ will ensure that we always place Him at the center of our journey; the gift of charity will enable us to deal with opposition and engage with others in a positive way. If we only try to think our way through our faith journey, we could be led astray. But with awakened spiritual gifts, we can proceed with the courage and confidence that Jesus's guiding hand is leading us along.

Aaron: Shortly after I was released as a bishop, Julie was called as a stake Relief Society president. This call came as a shock to her. She had served in several ward Relief Society presidencies as a counselor, but she had never served as a ward Relief Society president nor in any stake capacity. She reservedly accepted the call and began to serve. Nervous about her duties, she put her faith in Jesus and sought His will in everything she did.

During this period of service, I witnessed miracles occurring as the Savior caused hidden spiritual gifts and talents to come to light. Julie had always had a loving and kind nature, but her naturally compassionate disposition soared to new heights as she sought the Lord's help to meet the needs of over sixteen hundred sisters in our large and growing stake. As challenging and sometimes heartbreaking issues arose, she often felt impressed to pursue powerful and personal ministering in ways that I had not previously witnessed. The Lord was truly with her.

She was the presiding authority in her Relief Society presidency and a member of many stake presiding counsels, and I witnessed new leadership gifts emerge as the Lord unlocked them for her. She trained ward Relief Society presidencies, organized stake women's conferences, and worked with other stake Relief Society presidents to organize multi-stake events. In these many responsibilities, she developed into a useful leader among many other great women and men. Because she was a convert to the Church, this development was a miracle to me. Most of her peers had grown up having Church leadership modeled by their parents, whereas she had not. Yet the Lord helped her do things far above her skill set, and He qualified her for His work.

On one occasion, Julie was impressed to boldly suggest a change for a stake conference in which the Saturday evening session would be a series of workshops conducted by various members of the stake. She had identified numerous needs in her interviews with ward Relief Society presidents, and she had sought the Lord's guidance on how to meet them. She felt prompted that the needs could be addressed in these workshops. The stake presidency accepted this recommendation, and they assigned her to conduct the general evening session of stake conference. This heaven-led approach touched many of the women in our stake as it followed the pattern that the First Presidency had set in Saturday evening sessions of general conference by having sister leaders conduct.

Julie was never one who relished being in front of people. Yet the Lord knew that she had leadership skills that simply needed a catalyst to emerge. How grateful I was to be a witness to the blossoming that came under the Lord's direction. Like a butterfly that emerges from a cocoon, President Julie Bujnowski came forth from Sister Julie Bujnowski as the Lord blessed her with the opportunity to serve. Those hidden gifts advanced the Lord's work and blessed many lives, including hers.

Her faith in Jesus was the key that unlocked her hidden spiritual gifts. By navigating to Him, she became an effective instrument in His hand. I saw the words of Isaiah fulfilled in her: "[Jesus] hath made my mouth like a sharp sword; in the shadow of his hand hath he hid me, and made me a polished shaft; in his quiver hath he hid me."[138] Indeed, she became a polished shaft in the Lord's quiver that was hidden for use in His timing for His work because of her faith in Him.

We can have the same experience in our assigned field of labor as we put our faith in Jesus. He knows who we can become, and He will help us get there as He did for Julie.

ACKNOWLEDGING THE GOODNESS OF GOD

When we face opposition and progress through our stages of faith, we can become myopic in our view of life—narrowing our vision to only the trouble or questions we see immediately in front of us. When this occurs, we can fail to see God's hand in every aspect of our lives. We may believe He has forgotten us, or worse, that He doesn't exist at all. In other cases, we see the positive, but we attribute His blessings to our efforts instead of to His grace. This lack of vision is offensive to God. "In nothing doth man offend God, or against none is his wrath kindled, save those who confess not his hand in all things, and obey not his commandments."[139]

Confessing God's hand can mean recognizing He is there for us and wants the best for us, even if our current circumstances seem bleak and He seems distant. It could also mean attributing any blessings to His interventions even when our personal efforts have been significant. The power to carry out those efforts came from Him because He allowed us to experience mortality and gave us a Savior who could ensure that our insufficient efforts didn't prevent us from receiving all that He has.

When we awaken to His hand in our lives, we become grateful because we recognize that He blesses us far beyond what our natural talents would merit. Gratitude lifts us because it humbles us. Humility is an enabler of faith, hope, and, eventually, charity.[140] It will power us through our journey of faith and allow us to grow to new spiritual heights. Gratitude will lift us to greater levels of joy and happiness. As Elder Gary B. Sabin taught, "You will never be happier than you are grateful."[141]

Julie: Once Aaron and I had the occasion to meet with a sister who was preparing to return to the temple after a period of not attending. She had gone through a very painful divorce due to the abuse and infidelity of her husband. She was now raising her children as a single mother, trying to balance meeting their needs with finding healing for herself.

As we listened to her story, she shared with us all the miraculous ways that God had blessed her on her journey of faith. She went through dark periods of doubt and distress. Being divorced was a situation she never anticipated, and she found it difficult to attend church or even read her scriptures. She wondered if she would ever find happiness again and struggled to find meaning in what had happened, all of which was outside of her control. Although she stopped doing many things that an active believer would do, she never stopped praying. This connection to God was her lifeline.

In her pleadings with her Heavenly Father, she put on the altar all her pain and concerns. Most importantly, she looked for God's hand in her life as she waited on His blessings. Because of her connection to Him, she started to recognize the small miracles happening around her. And she acknowledged that these were blessings from God. Over time, attributing these small but positive events to Him caused her to strengthen her faith in Jesus and eventually to resume her activity in the Church.

Now she had her temple recommend once again, and she was excited to return to the House of the Lord to reexperience the joy of worshipping there. Her gratitude to God was undeniable. And this appreciation for Him was the anchor that stabilized her on her long and difficult journey back. Acknowledging God's goodness truly saved her, and it can save you and me.

IDENTIFYING GOD'S COMPENSATORY BLESSINGS

Compensatory blessings are those tender mercies that come to us in place of the blessings we may lose during our difficult times. We must always awaken to God's compensatory blessings when opposing forces come upon us because these difficulties may prevent us from receiving the blessing we originally sought. If we pay attention, we will witness God's hand in our lives as He brings forth new growth—new blessings in us and around us. Of these compensatory blessings, Elder Richard G. Scott taught us to

> find the compensatory blessings in your life when, in the wisdom of the Lord, He deprives you of something you very much want. To the sightless or hearing impaired, He sharpens the other senses. To the ill, He gives patience, understanding, and increased appreciation for others' kindness. With the loss of a dear one, He deepens the bonds of love, enriches memories, and kindles hope in a future reunion. You will discover compensatory blessings when you willingly accept the will of the Lord and exercise faith in Him.[142]

We can always find Jesus in opposition—if we look for Him. To Him, we should give gratitude during the opposition of ease. From Him, we receive comfort and guidance during the opposition of difficulty. God's blessings through His Son have an amplifying effect upon us. When we fight through ease or affliction, He will amplify our meager efforts. He will send us compensatory blessings when our desires do not align with His will.

Julie: Jennie Taylor's story is an example of awakening to compensatory blessings. As a mother of seven children, she lost her husband, Brent Russell Taylor, when he was killed during an overseas deployment in 2018. A young widow with seven children, she faced difficult days trying to cope with grief and working to make ends meet. In a touching video produced by The Church of Jesus Christ of Latter-day Saints, she shared her thoughts on the compensatory blessings she witnessed from this tragedy.

> In some of my darkest moments, some of my deepest anguish, I have come to believe that life is incredibly unfair *in our favor*. . . . I think it's important to recognize that even though we want everything to happen for a reason, it's probably a better mindset to *let God help make reason of everything that happens*. . . .
>
> Over the last three years, I have come to know [Jesus Christ] in a very intimate way. I know Jesus Christ is real. I know he's closer to me than I might think. I know He loves me, and He's aware of all of my weaknesses, and my fears, and my anxieties. And I know He's willing to walk with me

> hand-in-hand and make sure I can get through whatever it is I need to face in a day. . . .
>
> My husband's death has opened a lot of doors for me to be able to do God's will and help other people and learn and grow. And I think every day [about] how grateful I am that he would be willing to die for me. That's a pretty overwhelming statement to make—that my husband literally gave his life for me.[143]

We, like Jennie Taylor, can find compensatory blessings when we put Christ at the center of our lives. He will guide and comfort us through our opposing experiences of life. He will enable spiritual growth in us as those experiences come to us in God's wisdom. This is His way. He *is* the Way.

Those compensatory blessings may be delayed, but they will surely come. Among those blessings will be an awakening in our lives that will enable us to move forward spiritually and progress toward our mighty change of heart. It happened for Jennie Taylor, and it will happen for each of us as we keep our focus on Jesus Christ and awaken to His glorious and merciful blessings.

QUESTIONS TO CONSIDER

1. What barriers in your life might be preventing you from experiencing your spiritual awakening? How can you remove those barriers?
2. What new insights and awakenings have you recently had about yourself, your discipleship, and your Savior? How did this awakening happen? How can you continue this process in a positive way?
3. What stage of faith or growth are you currently in? How can your knowledge of and faith in Jesus Christ help you move forward through the other stages?
4. What spiritual gifts would allow you to awaken more completely? How could you better seek and develop them?
5. What compensatory blessings have you experienced in your life? How have they shown God's love for you?

NOTES AND INSIGHTS

3

KNOW GOD'S PLAN OF MERCY

And this is life eternal, that they might know thee the only true God, and Jesus Christ, whom thou hast sent.

—JOHN 17:3

Julie: In 1999 I became pregnant with our second child. Our oldest, Breanna, was a little over two years old, and we were excited to welcome a new little spirit into our home. This pregnancy was different than my first. With Breanna, I only had morning sickness through the first part of my pregnancy, but this time, I felt very sick nearly the entire time.

About seventeen weeks into my pregnancy, I went for a routine checkup with my obstetrician. I was sick again that morning, so nothing seemed unusual. However, during the visit, the faces of my clinicians became very solemn when they used a sonogram to check on the baby. They could not find a heartbeat.

I called Aaron at work and told him what was happening. He immediately met me at the doctor's office where my providers would perform more extensive tests. Those tests confirmed what was initially suspected—my baby had died.

This news broke our hearts. Only weeks before, we had heard a strong heartbeat at a doctor's visit, and we were excitedly preparing for the next phase of my pregnancy. Now, we faced the harsh reality that our baby would not be joining us in this life.

As we prepared for the procedure to remove the deceased baby, we felt strong emotions and asked ourselves important questions. Why had this happened? What could we have done to prevent it? How did this fit into God's plan for us? We had many questions but few answers.

We prayed and pondered. We asked Heavenly Father for comfort. We counseled with our bishop. We talked with friends and family, some of whom had experienced similar losses in their lives. Their expressions of compassion and empathy were helpful, but they didn't fully resolve our questions—or stanch the tears.

I was serving as our ward Primary president, so I heard the basic principles of the gospel taught each week at Church. I clung to those gospel fundamentals during this time: Jesus loved me; Heavenly Father had a plan for our family; I am a child of God.

I loved being a mother. I still do. My children are precious to me. This child—our little Angel—is equally as precious. In some ways, I still mourn for the premature loss of this baby. That hole in my soul remains. However, I have faith in my Savior and I believe in His plan.

Perhaps I'll never know precisely what happened to cause me to lose this child, and I don't fully understand how this loss fits into God's plan. But I trust His plan, which promises me that all will be made right in the eternities because of Jesus and His infinite Atonement.

My knowledge of God's plan of mercy and Jesus's central role in it has helped me move forward with hope. And this hope continues to sustain and comfort me through my loss.

This chapter focuses on knowing God's plan of mercy. When events in our lives create opposition or contrast that awakens us to God, we can often wonder how those occurrences fit into God's plan for us. Whether we're dealing with basic complexity or paralyzing perplexity, we frequently seek meaning in life's occurrences. Even if we don't yet know the meaning of specific events, we can always return to Heavenly Father's overarching plan for His children—the plan that was prepared and communicated from the foundation of the world—to frame what we have experienced against His greater purposes.[144] And this plan can help us navigate our faith journey with greater purpose and direction.

The Book of Mormon has nine names for God's plan.[145] The most frequent is the *plan of redemption*. Other names include *plan of salvation*, *plan of deliverance*, *plan of restoration*, and *plan of mercy*. These names explicitly state the intention of His plan: to help us qualify for mercy and escape the "grasp of justice."[146] God's plan was the blueprint for how He would enable His children to return to live with Him, fully prepared to join Him in His great eternal purpose to "bring to pass the immortality and eternal life of [all His children]."[147]

THE PLAN'S BASICS

The basic elements of God's plan of mercy are well taught in Church theology. We will only provide a brief synopsis here.[148] In the premortal world, our heavenly parents created us as Their spirit children and wanted to give us the opportunity to become like Them. To progress, we would need to acquire a physical body and have a set of experiences that would allow us to develop the characteristics of godliness They possessed: love, humility, meekness, kindness, patience, and all others. To qualify to live with God once again, we would need to remain perfect through the experiences of mortality because "no unclean thing can enter into his kingdom."[149]Our heavenly parents knew we could not receive a mortal body and have a mortal experience without imperfections. So, they chose a Savior—Jehovah, their most valiant spirit child—who willingly volunteered to come into mortality, live a perfect life, take upon Himself all our sins, transgressions, and sicknesses, then freely sacrifice Himself for us to satisfy the demands of justice.[150] This Holy One was born as Jesus of Nazareth—Jesus the Christ.

Upon completing His atonement—His suffering at Gethsemane, His sacrifice on the cross, and His resurrection at the tomb—He conquered both death and sin. As our Judge and Advocate, He could, then, offer us mercy if we choose to live His gospel law, which requires us to live the doctrine of Christ. This doctrine invites us to have faith in Jesus Christ, sincerely and regularly repent, be baptized, receive the gift of the Holy Ghost, and endure to the end. If we strive to live His doctrine, Jesus will offer us His mercy, and He will save us by His grace.[151]

Heavenly Father put His plan into place, but only after a rebellion saw one-third of the premortal hosts fight against it, led by Lucifer—now called Satan—the enemy of all righteousness. They were defeated by the word of our testimony[152] and were cast out and down to earth where they contribute to the opposition we face here. Satan and his fallen minions continue their fight against God and our agency, hoping to make "all men [and women] miserable like unto himself."[153] Agency was the core of the spiritual battle then, and it is the heart of our spiritual battles now. Why? Because choice is power, and Satan craves power and glory.[154]

The family has a central role in God's plan because it was designed to be the vehicle for welcoming God's children into mortality. As our modern prophets have declared, "The family is central to the Creator's plan for the eternal destiny of His children."[155] We can learn the principles of righteousness in the family, and, at its best, it can be a peaceful haven from the storms of mortal life.

IMPLICIT PRINCIPLES

Now, we live in mortality, experiencing God's plan. At times, our lives can seem to be going smoothly, and the Father's plan seems to be working for us. Other times, life is difficult, and the plan does not seem to be working. Doubts and questions may ensue, threatening to derail our faith.

To help us in these situations, we must not only understand the *explicit* elements of God's plan of salvation but also its *implications*. This understanding could help us to see the potential rationale for things that God does or doesn't do as we encounter opposition on our faith journey. We might suggest that there are five implicit principles that drive God's dealings with His children as He carries out His plan of mercy:

- He always acts out of love
- He always protects our agency
- He always safeguards the everlasting covenant

- He always blesses the greatest number of His children
- He always points His children to Jesus Christ

We discuss each of these principles below.

GOD ACTS OUT OF LOVE

First and foremost, we must understand that God always acts out of love for us—collectively and individually. If something happens in our lives that we don't fully comprehend, we can still know that He loves us. Nephi, when confronted with such an issue, eloquently stated, "I know that he loveth his children; nevertheless, I do not know the meaning of all things."[156] Like him, we should always know that Heavenly Father acts out of love even if we don't understand what He's doing to us and for us at the moment. This deep and eternal love drives everything God does to achieve His purpose of bringing to pass our immortality and eternal life.[157]

Heavenly Father may allow difficult things to happen because He wants us to progress. As we mentioned in a previous chapter, opposition paradoxically propels us forward. He may allow us to experience periods of doubt or confusion because He wants us to put in the work to seek Him and develop faith in His Son. These are acts of love. In the same way that a parent lets go of a toddling child as she learns to walk—even allowing her to stumble—our loving Heavenly Father guides us with wisdom and allows us to learn and progress through the ups and downs of mortality. We may not like this type of love, but we will always appreciate its ultimate effects.

Love is the reason God intervenes in our life, and it is the reason He withholds His hand. We must trust His eternal judgment in how He chooses to deal with circumstances that arise in our lives. As we do, we will develop a reciprocal love for Him. "We love him, because He first loved us."[158]

When Aaron and I lost the pregnancy, we did not know and still do not know the reasons it happened. However, we know with assurance that Heavenly Father loves us. We felt that love directly through His Spirit and indirectly through the ministering of the many who attended to our needs at that difficult time. His love was a salve to our souls and helped us heal. That love is available to all His children.

GOD ALWAYS PROTECTS OUR AGENCY

Second, we must understand that God will always protect and never violate our agency. Ever. Our agency was so precious to Him that He created a plan that would wholly and fully protect it, even if its design meant that some of His children would not return to Him because of their willing choices. He loved us enough to let us go.

The plan of salvation is founded on the freedom to make choices even when those choices are bad for us. God cannot always protect us from the consequences of our choices, but He defends our right to make them. What love! We can only imagine the sadness He feels when He witnesses the difficulty His children create for themselves. Many mortal parents experience this sadness as they witness the choices of their children. Yet He will not take away our freedom to choose. How does God's plan protect our agency?

First, giving commandments protects agency by providing choices. Without His commandments, we would not have the choice between obedience and disobedience; and a lack of choice compromises agency.[159] As the prophet Lehi taught, "Wherefore, the Lord God gave unto man that he should act for himself. Wherefore, *man* could *not* act for himself save it should be that he was *enticed by the one or the other*."[160] We can choose to obey or not to obey. Natural consequences follow each choice, but either way, we are free to choose.[161]

Second, Heavenly Father protects agency by delivering blessings via covenants. Covenants are two-way promises that create a new relationship between us and Him. Covenants must be entered into willingly by both parties, thereby protecting the agency of each. Blessings are only developed if we *choose* to keep them. Therefore, they are among God's most important protections of our agency.

Finally, the Savior's Atonement protects agency because through Him our poor choices will not forever condemn us. Were it not for Jesus Christ and His infinite Atonement, we could be afraid of making any choices for fear of making the wrong ones, forever condemning us to live outside of the Father's presence. However, through the precious gift of repentance, Jesus Christ can acquit us of the consequences of our choices. Jesus is the ultimate protector of agency.

GOD ALWAYS SAFEGUARDS THE EVERLASTING COVENANT

The third principle we must understand is that God will always protect the everlasting covenant. Because the covenant connects Him to us and simultaneously protects agency, He ensures that the covenant continues. In Old Testament times, He protected the covenant by ensuring that it was passed from parents to children within a covenant family—first through the family of Adam and then through the family of Abraham and the house of Israel. Outsiders could join that family, but covenant membership was highly restricted to those from this house. He also protected the covenant by ensuring that only His authorized messengers—the prophets—conveyed His messages to the covenant people.

Unfortunately, the fullness of the everlasting covenant was briefly lost and had to be restored. This Restoration occurred when Heavenly Father called a prophet for our day, Joseph Smith.[162] He and all subsequent prophets work under the direction of Jesus, for He fulfilled the covenant, and He ensures that it includes all of God's children on both sides of the veil.

Fortunately, the Savior commanded that the new and everlasting covenant be taken to the whole world.[163] Baptism joins us to Abraham's family and offers us entry to the new and everlasting covenant. Although it is now offered to everyone on both sides of the veil, God still must protect it. He continues to use authorized ministers to deliver the covenant and His messages, so we won't be deceived. He makes sure that His restored Church—the conveyor of the covenant—is not destroyed again through a general apostasy. And He ensures that the positions of precious keyholders (members of the Quorum of the Twelve Apostles) are always filled. This continuity of the covenant's keys is critical to its sustainability.

The covenant was largely lost during a time when people fell away from the gospel of Jesus Christ after the Apostles (His authorized messengers) were killed. It cannot be lost again now that it has been restored through the Prophet Joseph Smith.[164] The spiritual fate of the entire world depends on the success of this last dispensation. Therefore, we might suggest that many of the policies and practices in

His restored Church are intended to protect this sacred covenant. In His mercy, Jesus will ensure that any issues that occur when imperfect humans do His perfect work of protecting the covenant will be made right in the eternities.

GOD BLESSES AS MANY AS POSSIBLE

Fourth, we must understand that God will always strive to bless as many of His children as possible, within the limits their agency presents Him. He does this collectively and individually.

Collectively, to bless as much of the world as possible and still guard the covenant and His children's agency, Heavenly Father uses the process of scattering and gathering. His small family of covenant children is often scattered in various geographic locations, which "seed" those covenant children among other non-covenant people. After a period of growth and decline in these new geographies, God gathers them back into the fold, renewing their faith and their covenant with Him.[165] As President Russell M. Nelson declared, "[The] gathering is the most important thing taking place on earth today. Nothing else compares in magnitude, nothing else compares in importance, nothing else compares in majesty."[166]

Individually, God has the same desire to bless as many people as possible. We've often wondered if a delayed blessing is nothing more than Heavenly Father trying to arrange circumstances such that when we receive our desired blessing, others can receive theirs at the same time. Surely, heaven's ecology of blessings is efficient *and* effective, wasting as little effort as possible to bless as many as He can. Because divine delays require our faith, humility, and patience, His higher way further develops us even as He blesses us and others.

GOD ALWAYS POINTS US TO JESUS CHRIST

Finally, Heavenly Father will always point us to His Son. Jesus is the source of all mercy and all blessings. He is the One who can make right all unfairness that can occur as Heavenly Father protects our and others' agency, guards the covenant, and uses scattering, gathering, and divine delays to bless as many people as possible. Jesus is the great Equalizer. He is the merciful Redeemer. He is the loving Healer of hurts, wrongs, and any other unfairness earth-life may elicit. Jesus is always the answer for us through the Father.[167] So Heavenly Father always wants us to seek His son when we are faced with any question, doubt, or difficulty. Again, Jesus is always the answer!

Faith in Jesus Christ is the first principle of the gospel, so Heavenly Father will always seek to increase our faith in Jesus. If we don't receive the answer to an important question or if we don't experience the timely resolution to a difficulty, we might look for the way this challenge could enlarge our faith in Jesus Christ. Perhaps when we face complexity or are amid perplexity, faith in Jesus Christ is what God is developing in us.

JESUS IS THE CENTER OF THE PLAN

Often, when we describe Heavenly Father's plan of salvation, we share a narrative that follows the timeline-centered description shown in the figure below. We begin at our premortal existence, describe mortality, move on to death and our time in the spirit world, and then describe the final degrees of glory available to all except the sons of perdition. Although this narrative and its associated depiction is accurate, it leaves out the most important part of the plan—the Savior, Jesus Christ! We wondered, "What would a different depiction of the plan of salvation look like with the Savior at the center?" As we pondered, we studied many statements about God's plan by modern prophets and apostles. We thoroughly studied all the talks given by our current prophet, President Russell N. Nelson.

Based on our study, we developed a Christ-centered depiction that includes key elements of the timeline version, but it adds key actions, covenants, and objectives articulated by prophets, seers, and revelators throughout the ages.[168] What if we created depictions like this one to describe God's plan, which emphasize the centrality of Christ in it? How would they change our view of God's plan, and how would they strengthen our faith in Jesus Christ?

Just as Heavenly Father always points us to His Beloved Son, we should always focus on the Savior when we are moving through our stages of faith. Doing so will enable us to remain true and faithful to Jesus Christ and His restored gospel even when we face painful perplexity.

The Father gave us a singular command related to His Beloved Son: Hear Him![169] The Person at the center of the Father's plan should be the primary source of our spiritual information and guidance as we move through our stages of faith. How do we hear Him?

First, we can find the Savior's voice as we study the record of His teachings in the scriptures. Second, His voice is heard through the voice of His servants, for they are one and the same.[170] Finally, and most importantly, His voice comes to us directly via the Holy Spirit.

HIS VOICE THROUGH THE SCRIPTURES

We were taught in our youth that if we want to speak to our Heavenly Father, we should pray, and if we want Him to speak to us, we should read the scriptures. We have found this recommendation to be true. Whenever we read the scriptures, we find guidance for our lives

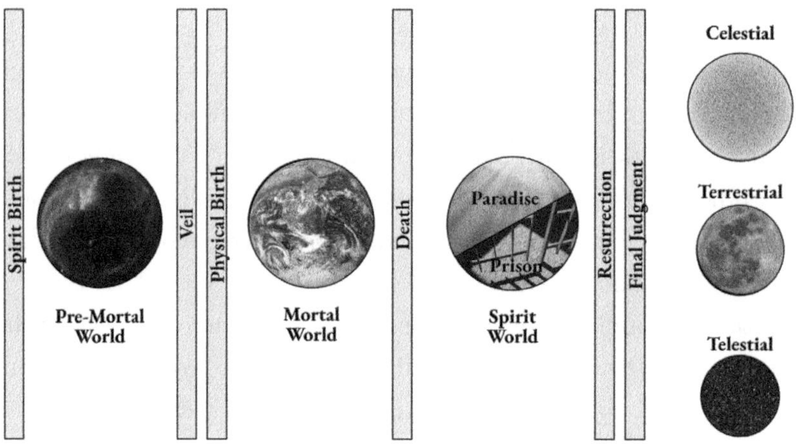

through their teachings. Individuals may debate the historical accuracy, doctrinal interpretation, or contextual application of various passages. However, when read with an open heart and a seeking mind, the scriptures can present us with information and inspiration that can guide us through our personal journey of faith.

We fear that too many who are struggling through their journey of faith leave the scriptures to seek answers elsewhere. Myriad resources can guide us during our times of complexity or perplexity. Some are helpful, and others are not. However, canonized scriptures are a constant source of God's voice. We would recommend that we always turn to them, even if we decide to search other sources. The scriptures will keep us close to our Heavenly Father and help us find Jesus.

Learning the language of the scriptures takes time and patience. Each person must pay the price of consistent reading, pondering, and

© Aaron & Julie Bujnowski

applying to have them become useful. Fortunately, the Church gives us access to many free resources that can help us with passages which are difficult to understand. If a specific phrase or verse isn't readily understandable and no resources are available to help, we would recommend moving on to a scripture that is more comprehensible.

As we study and ponder the scriptures, the Holy Spirit will touch our hearts and minds. He may simply provide a positive feeling that what we're reading is good, or we may receive a specific prompting. If no answers seem to come in the moment, perhaps the scripture we read will be needed later. Whatever the case, consistent work will result in improved understanding and application.

HIS VOICE THROUGH HIS SERVANTS

The Lord taught us, "Whether by mine own voice or by the voice of my servants, *it is the same*."[171] Who are these servants? They are the duly sustained, called, and set apart men and women who serve in various capacities in the Church. We might also add parents to this list as they preside in their homes. Each of these servants may receive inspiration and give counsel to the people over whom they have stewardship.[172]

We can read messages from the Church's general officers in the general conference reports. We hear from local leaders in conferences, sacrament meetings, classes, and councils. These individuals are imperfect, but they serve when they are called. When they speak, the Holy Spirit can confirm if what they are saying is from God and if it has application for us. If their recommendations lead us to Jesus and cause us to become and behave more like Him, then we will find joy and peace in following their counsel because we will know it is from God.

Unfortunately, not all experiences with counsel from the Lord's servants are positive. The imperfect human element can even affect someone whom God calls to serve. These imperfections have been the cause for many who struggle on their faith journey. The Lord knows that He must work through imperfect people to accomplish His perfect work, and He addressed this issue in the very first section of the Doctrine and Covenants.[173]

Fortunately, we don't believe negative experiences with Church leaders are the rule; they are generally the exception. When something negative has happened to us, we move on and eventually forget what happened. The Lord tells us, "If [the counsel or action] be not right you shall have no such [positive] feelings, but you shall have a stupor of thought that shall cause you to *forget the thing which is wrong*."[174] Unfortunately, some see leaders' imperfections as flaws in the Lord's work rather than flaws in the people doing it. We've been warned not to account the Lord's servants as a "light thing," for if we do, we may "stumble and fall when the storms descend, and the winds blow."[175]

Despite a few negative experiences with imperfect Church leaders, we have received overwhelmingly uplifting and helpful counsel from servants of God. We have been blessed as we have received wise and inspired counsel from general and local authorities throughout our lives. On more than one occasion, humble servants have blessed us with their words and actions. In most instances, their counsel was not directive, but it was instructive and encouraged us to follow the Holy Spirit's guidance. Sometimes, these individuals didn't know exactly why they had such an impact, but we knew. And we thanked our Heavenly Father for them. We can all have similarly positive experiences as we appropriately look to God's servants as part of our seeking process.

HIS VOICE THROUGH THE SPIRIT

The most important voice to hear and heed is God's voice speaking directly to us. The voice of the Holy Ghost is synonymous with God's voice, for the Holy Ghost is the channel through which God communicates with our minds and hearts.[176] As the Prophet Joseph Smith taught, the Holy Ghost may speak "pure intelligence" to our minds by giving us "sudden strokes of ideas."[177] Alternatively, He can speak to our hearts through the emotions of "love, joy, [and] peace" or by giving us the desire for greater amounts of the cardinal principles of "longsuffering, gentleness, goodness, faith, [or] meekness."[178]

Although there is some commonality in the way the Spirit communicates, everyone receives the impressions of the Spirit in a manner that is unique to them. Each must learn how we personally receive the guidance of heaven to make sure we recognize when the Holy Spirit speaks. We must learn for *ourselves* how these promptings feel.

The voice of the Spirit is still and small and can be easily missed or ignored if we are not paying attention or if we do not fully recognize that our thoughts and feelings are from above. Elder Boyd K. Packer taught us how to recognize the voice of the Holy Spirit when he said,

> [The] sweet, quiet voice of inspiration comes more as a feeling than it does as a sound. Pure intelligence can be spoken into the mind. The Holy Ghost communicates with our spirits through the mind more than through the physical senses. This guidance comes as thoughts, as feelings through promptings and impressions.[179]

If we recognize and receive the small amounts of inspiration the Lord gives us, He then provides us more, until our understanding is full.[180] This incremental method helps to humble us, to teach us patience, and to keep our "eye single"[181] to Him.

Aaron: My friend Tom had a powerful experience that taught him the importance of listening to Jesus.[182]

Tom and his wife adopted three beautiful children—two boys and girl—who were natural-born triplets. Through a series of miracles, they adopted the children and brought them back to their home in the United States.

These children loved their new life. They rode bikes, learned to ski, went to school, and did everything American children are privileged to do. Life was beautiful and happy. They were home, and they were loved.

However, after several years, their lives took a tragic turn. One of the boys got sick with what seemed to be a common virus. Thinking the treatment would be simple, their father took him to the hospital for treatment. While there, the child suddenly went into cardiac arrest. The virus, it seems, had gone to his heart, causing him to die of myocarditis.

Several months after his death, Tom and his wife were sitting on the couch crying and wondering why this tragedy had happened. Their other son, his twin brother, came up and asked why they were crying. They told him they didn't know why his brother had died and were wondering why it had happened.

This sweet, innocent child said, "Dad, the answer is simple: Jesus called my brother home, and he listened." He understood the simple principle that when Jesus talks, we should listen. These were wise and touching words from a faith-filled child. In them, Tom heard Jesus's voice comforting him.

We too can have this type of child-like faith when we face the challenge of complexity or perplexity. We can hear the Lord's voice calling us to Him if we listen. When we hear, then we can heed. Blessings always come when we heed Jesus's precious voice through the Holy Spirit.

GOD'S PLAN WORKS

With a firm knowledge of God's plan and Jesus's central role in it, we are better able to apply it in our lives, especially when we face difficult complexity or jarring perplexity. We know family and friends who have faced heartbreaking situations where God's plan doesn't seem to work for them. These experiences include an unexpected divorce, the death of a spouse, the challenge of finding an eternal companion, the inability to have natural born children, or being LGBTQ. For them, the blessings of God's plan seem unfairly distributed and unattainable. However, if we will persist, even when the plan seems "broken," we will be guided by the Lord to our promised land.

Elder Brook P. Hales shared a powerful experience that demonstrates an understanding of God's plan that will eventually come to faithful disciples of Jesus. Years earlier, he ministered to an older sister in his ward who had experienced a very difficult life. She had health issues, was divorced at age thirty-two, remarried, and was widowed at age sixty-six. After living for twenty-six years as a widow, she passed away. She stayed faithful to her testimony of Christ and to His Church until her death, despite her challenges. Shortly after her passing, her son was in the temple, and he had the experience of hearing his mother's voice in his mind. She said, "I want you to know that *mortality works*, and I want you to know that I now understand why everything happened [in my life] the way it did—and it is all OK."[183]

A widow in our ward communicated a similar sentiment in a sacrament meeting talk. She recounted losing her husband suddenly when he succumbed to the Texas heat while working outside. As she pondered the difficulty of what happened, she came to the following conclusion: "The Lord has a plan. I might not have a plan, but He does. I might not know where I fit in, but He does. And that's enough for me."[184]

Mortality works. God's plan works even when we face less than ideal situations. Perhaps understanding His plan—including the ideal definition of family—enables those of us for whom the plan *is* working to have a greater amount of compassion and empathy towards those who face challenging situations. Then we will be able to authentically love God and love our neighbor.

Knowing God's plan of mercy provides a framework for understanding and for ministering. It provides purpose and perspective. Most importantly, His plan provides a path for our journey of faith.

QUESTIONS TO CONSIDER

1. How can I know that God loves me despite my current situation? How can I feel that love now?
2. How has my agency or the agency of others been protected by what has happened?
3. How can I find Jesus in the experience I'm having? How can I Hear Him and feel His guiding hand?
4. How would you draw the plan of salvation with Jesus at the center? Create your own version of the plan and see how that helps you to focus on Him.
5. What can you do to navigate to Jesus when God's plan doesn't seem to be working for you?

NOTES AND INSIGHTS

4
SEEK THIS JESUS

I would commend you to seek this Jesus of whom the prophets and apostles have written, that the grace of God the Father, and also the Lord Jesus Christ, and the Holy Ghost, which beareth record of them, may be and abide in you forever.

—ETHER 12:41

Aaron: I attended high school in Nashville, Tennessee. The city is in an area of the United States known as the Bible Belt because of the Christian denominations that fervently focus on Bible teachings. This biblical loyalty is particularly prominent in Nashville, often called the Buckle of the Bible Belt.

In the late 1980s, I was one of only a handful of members of the Church of Jesus Christ in a high school of over twelve hundred students, so my Protestant classmates often asked me questions about my faith. These questions usually intensified after their local congregations held meetings and rallies specifically designed to oppose our Church doctrine.

I knew exactly what would happen at school the day after a rally. When I went to the lunchroom, I would be confronted by classmates who had information and literature they wanted to share with me.

Some were genuinely interested in my views, while others wanted to argue. This pattern repeated throughout my four years of high school.

I often took their information and read it. They highlighted issues such as Joseph Smith's polygamy, the past priesthood restriction for Black members, anachronisms in the Book of Mormon, the peculiarity of temple ceremonies, and the distinctiveness of our doctrine regarding the premortal existence, the three degrees of glory, and eternal families. Though less sophisticated than the information distributed via the internet, the topics were the same as we see repeated now by opponents of the Church.[185]

This information often caused me to have questions. When I searched for answers, I spoke to my father who was a convert to the Church. When he didn't have answers, he connected me to leaders in our stake who were more knowledgeable, like our stake patriarch and a member of our stake presidency who was a Church Educational System employee. They patiently and kindly listened to my questions, responded, and gave me new things to think about.

During this period, my father often told me, "You will have to find out for yourself whether the things we believe are true. I can't do that for you. Do your research. Pray and ask Heavenly Father for His guidance. Then, you can decide to stay in the Church or leave based on what you find. The decision is yours, just like it was for me when I joined the Church." He wisely encouraged me to have a personal conversion experience rather than to depend on his.

In all my seeking and asking, I realized that Jesus was always the center of my search. I could find peace when I focused on Him regardless of the issue or doubt I was trying to resolve. In the years that have followed, this truth has become more apparent to me: Jesus is the first and best answer to every spiritual question I may have. This discovery became my spiritual foundation, a foundation that would help me when I experienced other, more severe difficulties later in life.[186]

In this chapter, we will discuss the critical need to seek Jesus on our journey of faith. Faith journeys nearly always entail seeking. When we face opposition and are trying to understand God's plan, we look for truth, comfort, connection, meaning, and purpose. Ultimately, we search for God. Authentic spiritual searching is healthy because it causes us to open our minds and hearts to new information, points of view, and hopefully, the influence of God through His Holy Spirit.

Although we may seek many different things on our faith journey, we must always seek this Jesus. He should be the center of our spiritual search because all things point to Him.[187] Any question can be answered by Him, through Him, in Him, and of Him. He has promised, "Ye shall seek *me*, and find *me* when ye shall search for *me* with all your heart"[188]

Julie and I currently teach our ward's temple preparation class. We tell our students that if they encounter a teaching or symbol in the temple that they don't fully understand, they should consider how it relates to Jesus, His Atonement, and His mission. We promise them that their answer will emerge while focusing their search on Jesus Christ. The same is true of any spiritual search.

We must seek Jesus to experience positive spiritual growth as we move through our stages of faith. Without Him, we take our hands off the iron rod on our journey and can eventually become "lost," "wandering in strange roads."[189] With Him, we can remain safely on His path of salvation because our journey of faith follows the strait and narrow path He laid out for us. Jesus must become the center of all we do and all we are as individuals, as families, and as a Church body. As Nephi admonished, "The *right* way is to believe in Christ."[190]

The revised *Teaching in the Savior's Way* manual instructs us to have a central emphasis on Jesus Christ in our formal lessons.[191] However, we would suggest that this essential principle should extend to all we do in our lives. Perhaps, this manual could be called not just *Teaching in the Savior's Way* but *Leading in the Savior's Way*, *Parenting in the Savior's Way*, and, ultimately, *Living in the Savior's Way*. What is this way? Jesus is the Way.

When we have doubts or face difficult, complex, or even perplexing questions or situations on our faith journey, we should look for ways in which Jesus answers them through His teachings and life. This focus is not a cop-out; it is an act of faith in Him. Looking to Jesus can help us find our most important spiritual answers. And when we don't receive an answer now, or perhaps ever in this life, having faith in Jesus amid our unknowns will give us the patience and endurance we need to move forward anyway.

When we serve in the Church, everything we do should be focused on Christ. Every talk or lesson, no matter the topic, must be connected to Jesus Christ. If we talk of faith, we should always talk of faith in Jesus Christ. If we discuss repentance, we should talk about Jesus Christ's mercy in forgiving us. If we teach about the covenant path, we should teach the Savior's role in that covenant. If we talk of self-reliance, we should speak of how the Savior sustains us in that effort and how being self-reliant will enable us to serve Him more effectively. If we talk of missionary work, we should discuss bringing people to Jesus Christ via covenants.

When we are at work, in the community, or at school, we should likewise make choices that align with what the Savior would do, and ultimately, be. If we face a seemingly impossible issue or a heartbreak of unfathomable magnitude in any aspect of our lives, we should turn to Jesus Christ for help, healing, guidance, and direction. We should seek Him when we wrestle with our faith, for He is the One in whom we should have faith. We should center on Jesus when we receive precious spiritual or temporal blessings, for this focus will help us remain humble and meek by recognizing that He was their source. We should always put Jesus Christ at the center of all our intentions, considerations, and actions. Again, He *is* the Way.

Perhaps we think of ourselves as people who are also disciples of Christ. We may see ourselves as an "employee who is a disciple of Christ," an "elementary school teacher who is a disciple of Christ," or a "community volunteer who is a disciple of Christ." We recommend flipping that emphasis. We are disciples of Jesus Christ who also have other roles. With this properly aligned emphasis, we should think of ourselves as "a disciple of Christ who is an employee," "a disciple of Christ who is an elementary school teacher," or "a disciple of Christ who is a community volunteer." Having a Christ-centered framing makes our covenant discipleship of Jesus the center of our choices and intentions, with everything else revolving around it.

We should understand and always remember that Jesus Christ directs all aspects of the Father's work, so He must be the center of all we do and ultimately, all we are. For example, when we humbly pray to our Father in Heaven, the Father deploys the Savior to direct the work of answering our prayers. The Savior actively ensures that "all things shall work for [our] good."[192] He may use many seen and unseen servants in accomplishing the Father's will for us, but the Savior is at the helm. When we recognize this sublime fact, our love for Him will abound, even as His love for us is without limits.

Jesus Christ should be the center of all we do in every aspect of our lives. Other important considerations take our time, but none should supplant our focus on the Savior. Nothing should distract us from our primary focus: Him. If we take our eye off Him, we will not stand on a firm foundation, and we will eventually fall. But, if we build our lives on Jesus Christ, we "cannot fall."[193]

As Elder Neal A. Maxwell so eloquently taught, "My fellowmen [and women, girls, boys, and youth], it matters so very much how we regard and view Jesus Christ. Some seek to substitute Caesars for Christ. Others are blinded because they are 'looking beyond the mark'[194] when the mark is Christ."[195]

We should never look beyond that divine mark—Jesus of Nazareth, Savior and King. We will stumble if we are not founded on Christ. We will wrestle with truth, be overcome by our trials, and be hindered on our covenant path if our faith is not centered on Him—on Jesus, our Lord and Master.[196] Therefore, we should always focus on the "author and finisher of our faith,"[197] our Advocate with the Father,[198] our Savior and Redeemer—Jesus the Christ. He is "the great, and the last, and the only sure foundation, upon which [we] can build."[199]

As we seek Jesus by centering ourselves on Him, we recommend understanding and following His invitations and admonitions as recorded in the scriptures. Below we will briefly address each of His inspired invitations to put Him at the center of our lives, and we will summarize how to accept and act on them. His invitations are to *Follow me; Come unto me; Ask of me; Believe me; Receive me; Abide in me*, and *Rejoice in me.*

If we do these things, His promise is, "I will come unto you."[200] As we heed His invitations, we will be more capable of navigating our faith journey—especially when that journey takes us through periods of difficulty, doubt, or uncertainty. Why? Jesus comes to us as we center ourselves on Him. Let's consider each of His loving invitations together.

FOLLOW ME

Jesus invited many to follow Him during His mortal ministry. We summarize them below in the approximate order in which they occurred in the four gospels.

At the beginning of His ministry, as Jesus gathered the men who would become His Apostles—His closest and most trusted followers—He bade them with a simple invitation: "*Follow me*,"[201] adding to those who were fishermen, "and I will make you fishers of men."[202] These men left their professions and personal interests and followed the Master. As other women and men also sought ways to become disciples, Jesus extended this same invitation to them.

To the person who wanted to bury his father before becoming a disciple, Jesus said, "*Follow me*; and let the dead bury their dead."[203] Later, when some disciples wanted Jesus to plainly declare that He was the Christ, He said, "I told you, and ye believed not. . . . My sheep hear my voice, and I know them, and they *follow me*."[204]

When Jesus taught His Apostles that he would suffer and die, and Peter rejected this idea, the Savior rebuked him and taught, "If any man will come after me, let him deny himself, and take up his cross, and *follow me*. For whosoever will save his life shall lose it: and whosoever will lose his life for my sake shall find it."[205]

To the rich young ruler who desired to know how to gain eternal life but who loved his riches more than his discipleship, Jesus said, "If thou wilt be perfect, go and sell that thou hast, and give to the poor, and thou shalt have treasure in heaven: and come and *follow me*."[206]

Just before Jesus's crucifixion, two Greeks had come seeking Jesus (at the feast) to become His disciples. Andrew and Phillip came to Jesus to tell Him of their interest in His ministry. Sensing that the Greeks and His apostles did not understand the full weight of Christian discipleship, Jesus taught them of His impending death and then said, "He that loveth his life shall lose it; and he that hateth his life in this world shall keep it unto life eternal. If any man serve me, *let him follow me*."[207]

Finally, following Jesus's resurrection, He met with His Apostles at the Sea of Galilee, where they had gone fishing instead of tending to their ministry. After inviting Peter to "feed my sheep,"[208] Peter asked about John's future mission. Gently rebuking Peter for not focusing on his own mission, the Savior said, "If I will that [John] tarry till I come, what is that to thee? *Follow thou me*."[209] Jesus ended His mortal ministry as He began, with a simple invitation to follow Him.

Following Jesus Christ means to live in a way that reflects His teachings, values, and example. For Christians, following Jesus is a personal commitment to a life centered on love, sacrifice, and service to others. We follow Jesus by doing what He did and ultimately, by becoming as He is.[210]

We would suggest that each of Jesus's invitations represents a category of action in following Him. These choices are critical when traversing our journey of faith, especially when that journey becomes difficult, complex, or paradoxical. Let's learn about them so we can apply them on that journey.

First, we are to leave behind our personal interests and biases as did the disciples who left their professions to follow Him. Not all will become full-time ministers like the early Apostles, but all disciples of Jesus must sacrifice their interests to serve Him.

Second, we are not to prioritize things of earthly importance like the would-be disciple who wanted to care for his dead before following the Master. Harmonizing myriad demands on our time can be challenging, but choices related to our Christian discipleship should be appropriately ordered. When we put Jesus first as often as possible, we signal to Him that we are willing to learn, which will open the windows of heaven to us.

Third, as the rich young ruler was taught, we are to use our means and excess to bless the poor and needy, focusing on their well-being. We might not be asked to give away all (as he was), but we are asked to sacrifice at least a portion of our means for the benefit of others. Focusing on others leads us to forget about our own doubts and difficulties. This expanded perspective can help shatter our spiritual, self-centered myopia and help us become open to greater gospel truths.

Fourth, we must be willing to sacrifice our good name, our reputation, and our very lives if necessary to follow Jesus. Discipleship is meant to be an *all-in* activity, and the Lord recognizes our level of commitment. He reciprocates what we give—eventually. The Lord requires continued commitment for His most precious blessings.

Finally, we must not worry about what discipleship looks like for others—only what it looks like for us. Comparison is the thief of joy and nowhere is this axiom truer than in Christian discipleship. When we worry or obsess about how seemingly easy another person may have found answers to questions or developed a testimony of truth, we can become dissatisfied with our situation. We may not realize the price the other person had to pay to make difficult things appear to be easy, and we may choose not to pay that price ourselves. How tragic it would be to walk away from a spiritual search just when the incline began to steepen only to find that this challenge was the very thing that could generate the faith we desired.

We are not suggesting that doing these five things to follow Jesus will remove all doubt or resolve all paradoxes. However, pursuing them authentically and with measured intensity will enable those who truly want to find answers from God to be in a much better position to discover them—or at least not to be derailed by difficulties encountered in their search. Blessings always attend us when we follow Jesus.

COME UNTO ME

The second invitation that the Savior issued to all His disciples was "Come unto me." With this plea, He invites His followers to find rest, peace, and spiritual relief in Him. This invitation is deeply personal and offers comfort to those who feel burdened, weary, or overwhelmed by life's struggles. Jesus's call to "come" is an invitation to enter a close, personal relationship with Him and leave behind anything else. His call means turning to Him for guidance, strength, and connection, acknowledging Him as the ultimate source of love and support. "*Come unto me*, all ye that labour and are heavy laden, and *I* will give you rest."[211]

Jesus also invited, "Let the little children *come to me*, and do not hinder them, for the kingdom of heaven belongs to such as these."[212] Jesus loved the children. Their innocence and humility were meant to be a model for all Jesus's disciples. We are invited to come to Jesus the same as children: trusting fully, having no guile, being completely grateful, and always submitting to His will. Children are model disciples of the Master.

Jesus declared, "I am the bread of life. Whoever *comes to me* will never go hungry,"[213] and "If any man thirst, let him *come unto me*, and drink."[214] He invites any who are spiritually malnourished or dehydrated to come to him for nourishment. When we recognize that anything we lack can be provided by Him, we will willingly come to Him by accepting His gospel, making His covenants, developing His traits, and seeking His hope and healing.

LEARN OF ME

Jesus invited His disciples, "*Learn of me*; for I am meek and lowly in heart: and ye shall find rest unto your souls."[215] Learning of Jesus means becoming familiar with Him, not just memorizing His teachings. We can learn of His character, His actions, and His motivations. When we learn of Him, we can more easily love and, eventually, emulate Him.

Jesus is more profound and multifaceted than some might imagine. He lived perfectly, but His life, teachings, and example were not without complexity and paradox. His life was not simple, although we know the straightforward fact that He was the Son of God and our Redeemer. The life and actions of Jesus reflect a dialectical[216] nature as He embodied both divine authority and human vulnerability, challenging social norms while fulfilling the law through love and grace. These are examples of Jesus's intricacy that we must learn.

- He socialized with innocent children[217] and with sinners, outcasts, and social pariahs[218]
- He freely forgave sinners[219] yet harshly condemned hypocrites[220]
- He obeyed civil law[221] yet organized an unauthorized religious movement[222]
- He strictly complied with Mosaic law[223] but denounced man-made standards of behavior[224]
- He loved His mother[225] but broke her heart with His mission[226]
- He called authorized ministers to lead His perfect work[227] but allowed them to make mistakes in His service[228]
- He received saving ordinances even when He didn't need them[229]

- He called His disciples friends and loved them tenderly[230] yet corrected them sharply when they made mistakes[231]
- He taught hard sayings[232] that would divide families[233] yet He called for unity[234]
- He submitted to God's will, even when He preferred a different way[235]
- He learned and grew[236] but was perfect in avoiding temptation[237]
- He ministered, even when it broke social convention[238]
- He gave His life freely for others, even those who were His enemies and rejected Him[239]
- He humbly sought strength from His Father despite His tremendous spiritual gifts[240]
- He cared for the poor and needy and commended others to do the same[241] yet rejoiced when they paid their alms[242] and approved when resources were used to worship Him instead of helping them[243]
- He healed those who believed, even if they were ungrateful[244]
- He included women in His closest circles despite their lower social standing[245]
- He showed force[246] yet advocated for peace and forgiveness[247]

Elder Jeffrey R. Holland spoke of our need to understand the completeness and complexity that is Jesus.

> Down through history many have simplified, even trivialized our image of Him and His witness of who He was. They have reduced His righteousness to mere prudishness, His justice to mere anger, His mercy to mere permissiveness. We must not be guilty of such simplistic versions of Him that conveniently ignore teachings we find uncomfortable. This "dumbing down" has been true even regarding His ultimate defining virtue, His love.[248]

When we learn of Him, we come to appreciate this complexity, which helps us better understand how to live our lives and ultimately become like Him as we walk our complex and perplexing journey of faith.

ASK OF ME

Jesus invited His disciples, "*Ask of me* whatsoever thou wilt, and I will give it thee."[249] This invitation can be confusing for many who have asked for things they aren't granted. Loved ones die instead of recovering, jobs are lost instead of retained, or children rebel instead of obeying. Two factors are critical in Jesus's promise: God's will and others' agency. We might add a phrase to Jesus's invitation: "Ask of me whatsoever thou wilt, and I will give it thee [if God wills and if others' agency allows].[250]

The fact that God's will and others' agency must align for our petitions to be answered should not deter us in our efforts to ask. In Jesus's parable of the unjust judge,[251] a widow makes an extended plea to be avenged of her adversary. The wicked judge, wearied with her pleading, declares, "Because this widow troubleth me, I will avenge her, lest by her continual coming she weary me."[252] If an unrighteous judge would grant the widow her wishes, how much more will God, our loving Father, grant the desires of His children if we are persistent in our righteous requests?

Jesus's invitation to ask is His encouragement to elevate the intensity and longevity of our spiritual requests. We must not become weary in our petitioning. Why would He not readily and easily grant our desires? Because He loves us, and He wants us to pay the price for things that are most precious to us. Only then will we develop the cardinal traits that enable us to become like our heavenly parents. His invitation to ask is an encouragement to *become*.

BELIEVE ME

Jesus bade His disciples to "*Believe me* that I am in the Father, and the Father in me: or else *believe me* for the very works' sake."[253] Jesus did not say "Believe *in* me." He said, "Believe me." Believing Jesus means that we accept and trust what He teaches, we faithfully follow His invitations, and we accept His testimony of His mission as Savior and Redeemer.

First, Jesus asks us to believe that He is unified with the Father—that all He teaches and represents leads us back to Heavenly Father. Therefore, when we want to find God, we must seek Jesus. Second, He asks us to believe Him "for the very works' sake." If His gospel is to be taken to "all nations"[254] as Jesus commanded in His "great commission," then His disciples must believe Him, trusting that His gospel will heal hearts, save souls, comfort heartaches, and sanctify sin.

Some stop believing Jesus when their faith journey becomes difficult and mired in perplexity. They stop trusting His teachings and His testimony. However, if we "believe Him," we can press forward to the harmony we seek. Don't stop believing.

RECEIVE ME

Jesus told His disciples, "Whosoever shall *receive me*, receiveth not me, but him that sent me."[255] We receive the Savior when we accept His role as Savior and Redeemer, internalize and live His doctrine, and welcome His presence into our lives via covenant.

First, accepting Jesus's role as Savior and Redeemer means that we allow His grace to work for us and for others. The difficulty that we experience can lead us to become jaded as a never-ending stream of challenges can seem unfair, unjust, and unnecessary. However, when we accept Jesus, understanding that His "grace is sufficient,"[256] we can know that these difficult things will all be resolved in Him, through Him, and by Him.

Second, living Jesus's doctrine is an important way to receive Him. His doctrine states that we should have faith in Him, repent of our sins, receive the covenant of baptism, receive the gift of the Holy Ghost, and endure to the end by doing all He asks, overcoming by faith any obstacles. His simple yet challenging doctrine is a pathway of safety for disciples of Christ.

Finally, the covenant path is an incremental process of receiving Jesus's presence. Covenants are not just two-way voluntary contracts; they form a new relationship. In this relationship, we voluntarily bind ourselves to Christ, and He reciprocates by binding Himself to us. Covenants are a formal way to mediate the Savior's grace. Willingly received and faithfully kept, covenants open the door to all Jesus's precious blessings. "Behold, I stand at the door, and knock: if any man hear my voice, and *open the door*, I will come in to him, and will sup with him, and he with me."[257]

ABIDE IN ME

Jesus commanded, "*Abide in me*, and I in you. As the branch cannot bear fruit of itself, except it abide in the vine; no more can ye, except ye *abide in me*."[258] To "abide" is "to continue without fading or being lost."[259] To abide in Jesus is to remain with Him and not run away—especially when life or Christian discipleship is difficult. Elder Jeffrey R. Holland taught,

> "Abide in me" is an understandable and beautiful enough concept in the elegant English for the King James Bible, but "abide" is not a word we use much anymore. So I gained even more appreciation for this admonition from the Lord when I was introduced to the translation of this passage in another language. In Spanish that familiar phrase is rendered "*permaneced en mi*." Like the English verb "abide," *permanecer* means "to remain, to stay," but even [English-speakers] like me can hear the root cognate there of "permanence." The sense of [the word abide], then, is "stay—but stay *forever*."[260]

During His ministry, Jesus faced an experience when some of His disciples decided to "walked no more with Him" because He had taught them "hard sayings."[261] To His closest followers (His twelve Apostles), Jesus asked, "Will ye also go away?"[262] Peter, the chief Apostle, spoke for the group, saying, "To whom shall we go? thou hast the words of eternal life. And *we believe and are sure* that thou art that Christ, the Son of the living God."[263]

The Apostles abided; they remained with Jesus, their Lord and Savior despite difficult teachings or any other opposing force or influence. We, too, can abide in Jesus during our journey of faith. Even if we doubt, we can remain until those doubts are somehow overcome through Him.

REJOICE WITH ME

One of Jesus's notable parables is often called "the parable of the lost sheep."[264] In this story, a shepherd leaves ninety-nine sheep to go after the one lost sheep. Upon finding it and returning home, the shepherd joyfully calls together his friends and neighbors and says, "Rejoice with me; for I have found my sheep which was lost.[265]

We prefer to call this story "the parable of the compassionate shepherd" because that title emphasizes the role and character of the shepherd rather than the condition of the sheep. Jesus wants us to rejoice with Him when anyone—including ourselves—is found. Being "found" may not be a singular event as portrayed in this parable. Our experience is that finding our way on our faith journey is a series of small acts. At each stage, whether for ourselves or others, we should rejoice with the Savior who finds joy in our spiritual progress. Rejoicing in our little wins together with the Savior will eventually result in a final "win" when we eventually come to our spiritual home with Jesus. Then, what was lost will truly be found.

I WILL COME UNTO YOU

In His Last Supper with the Twelve, Jesus gave them His final discourse. Among the many profound things He taught, He made this wonderful promise: "I will not leave you comfortless: *I will come to you.*"[266] These Apostles—the Savior's friends—may not have fully grasped the importance of His promise, not fully understanding that His death and their persecution for His name's sake was imminent.

Jesus had always offered His disciples words of encouragement, emotional assurance, and spiritual inspiration. "Be of good comfort," He said to the woman who had been cleansed from her issue of blood.[267] However, on this final occasion, after promising them, "I will come unto you," Jesus emphasized His commitment to their consolation:

> "If a man love me, he will keep my words: and my Father will love him, and *we will come unto him*, and *make our abode with him*."[268]

> "Peace I leave with you, my peace I give unto you: not as the world giveth, give I unto you. *Let not your heart be troubled, neither let it be afraid.*"[269]

> "Nevertheless I tell you the truth; *It is expedient for you that I go away*: for if I go not away, the Comforter will not come unto you; but if I depart, *I will send him unto you*. . . . Howbeit when he, the Spirit of truth, is come, *he will guide you into all truth*: for he shall not speak of himself; but whatsoever he shall hear, that shall he speak: and *he will shew you things to come*."[270]

Jesus promised comfort and peace. He gave assurances that He would be with His disciples in person or through the Holy Spirit. He promised that they would be guided to all truth. He did *not* promise resolution to their problems, only that they should not fear because He would provide peace in times of trouble.

We believe that Jesus anticipated that we would face difficulties on our faith journey. He knew that discipleship would be hard, so He promised that He would be with us on that path either personally or through His Spirit. The knowledge of His promise to abide with us—to stay with us forever—should calm our fears, lessen our anxiety, and give us hope. And that hope through Christ will sustain us on our journey of faith if we will but seek this Jesus.

Aaron: On a Sunday evening in late February 2014, I was called as bishop of a large and growing ward. Excited and nervous, I wanted to get a fast start on this important new assignment. However, my world was about to be turned upside down.

On Tuesday afternoon, I received a frantic call from my mother. In tears, she told me that my father had experienced some type of cardiac event at work. She was attempting to get details on his condition, but she could not get in touch with the hospital where he was taken. She did not know if he was dead or alive.

When she finally contacted the hospital, she was told that my father had a heart attack while at a training meeting. He had left the room and collapsed in the hallway. Miraculously, a co-worker who followed him out and saw him fall called for help, and he and another person administered CPR and used an automated external defibrillator until the paramedics arrived. At the hospital, the medical staff determined that my father had several blockages, and his prognosis was not good.

I immediately booked travel to be with my family. I told my new bishopric counselors about my family emergency and asked them to preside in my absence. I left the next day, knowing I would miss my first Sunday as bishop.

I arrived in Seattle and rushed to the hospital with my sister, where I learned that my father's condition had not improved. We were told that more than thirty minutes had passed before the paramedics could get him to the hospital. He was in a coma, and they did not know if he would survive.

The next morning while eating breakfast, we heard a "code blue" announced for my father's room. We rushed up from the cafeteria and saw the clinical team frantically working on him while alarms blared from the machines. A nurse was sitting on his chest administering CPR while the doctor barked out orders to other clinicians. My mother, brother, sister, and I stood outside the room in shock. A chaplain arrived and stood with us as we observed this surreal scene. The doctor commanded that one last medicine be administered, and finally, his heart started. They had averted another crisis.

The doctor counseled with us afterward. He told us that my father's chances of survival were very low due to the original cardiac event, the extended CPR, and this latest cardiac event. They were going to try a blood transfusion to take the load off his heart with freshly oxygenated blood and see if he would stabilize. That evening, my father's stake president arrived at the hospital. They knew each other because my father served as a high priest group leader. He spent a little time alone with my unconscious father, then came to chat with the family. He told us that he felt like it was not time for my father to pass.

The stake president's words comforted me, but I didn't believe him. I went home that evening pondering his promise. I knelt and prayed fervently for a miracle, not knowing if one would be granted. I read my scriptures, focusing on the Savior's Atonement and Resurrection. I sought Jesus. With this crisis, the stakes were much higher than when I had sought Him in high school when faced with anti-Church information. This emergency was life-threatening, and I needed Jesus more than ever.

The next day, I went to the hospital to be with my father. As I arrived, my brother called me with miraculous news—Dad had woken up! We rushed upstairs to see him. Dad looked at me, and I asked if he recognized me. He nodded his head. We asked him to squeeze our hands and wiggle his feet, which he did. We had received our miracle! Dad continued to make progress through the following week, getting stronger each day. My birthday occurred while I was in Seattle with him, and I rejoiced for the great blessing that I could celebrate with him.

My father went on to live an additional seven years until another heart attack finally took him in 2021. On that occasion, I similarly prayed for his recovery, but my petition was not granted. He was gone.

During the fateful week in 2014, I had made the following entry in my journal: "I have felt the strength and the watchful guidance of the Lord throughout this process. It has been a testimony builder to me of the power of prayer, faith, and priesthood blessings."

In 2021 on the day after his passing (Easter Sunday), I added the following entry: "I have a firm testimony of the living reality of our Savior, Jesus Christ. It is through Him that we can have a firm hope of seeing my father once again. The pain is still great, but hope takes the sting out of death. I never really understood that word 'sting' until now. His death does sting. It hurts. But like the pain from a slap, it dissipates quickly due to our faith in Christ."

Because I sought Jesus in my extremity, I found strength and comfort. In 2014, I did not know whether the outcome would be positive, but my faith in Jesus gave me the strength to endure that trial. In 2021, when the outcome was not positive, I still felt comfort and strength in Christ. I sought Jesus, and He came to me. He continues to be with me each time I seek Him in faith.

Like the prophet Moroni, I commend you to "seek this Jesus." If you do, He will come to you on your faith journey as He came to me on mine.

QUESTIONS TO CONSIDER

1. In what ways can you seek Jesus in your daily life?
2. What does the Savior's invitation "follow me" mean to you? What

are ways you can better follow the Savior? How can you come unto Him?

3. How can you learn more of the Savior? What would an increased knowledge of His traits, life, and teachings do for your discipleship? How could this understanding help you on your journey of faith?
4. How can you improve your ability to ask for and receive the Lord's blessings in your life? What can you do to accept the Lord's will for you, especially when His will is not yours?
5. What prevents you from believing the Savior? What is keeping you from abiding in or remaining with Him? How can you remove those barriers in your life?
6. What does Jesus's promise "I will come to you" mean to you? How has He come to you in the past? How might you anticipate He could come unto you in the future?

NOTES AND INSIGHTS

5

JUST BELIEVE ON HIM

As soon as Jesus heard the word that was spoken,
he saith unto the ruler of the synagogue,
Be not afraid, only believe.

—MARK 5:36

Julie: Aaron and I started dating in high school. After graduation in 1989, he attended BYU while I attended Middle Tennessee State University (MTSU). After we were apart one year, Aaron left for his mission to Concepción, Chile, where he would spend the next two years. I attended MTSU and worked while he served.

These were times before texting, email, and the internet, so all our communications were either by letter or, while we were in college, by phone. We had talked about getting married through our three-year courtship, and we continued the discussion in our letters during his mission.

About halfway through his time in Chile, Aaron wrote a letter asking me to marry him when he got home. I excitedly agreed and began preparing for our wedding. I believed our marriage would work. We were both faithful Latter-day Saints who believed in the importance of having an eternal marriage. Despite the doubts expressed by friends and family about how we would get ready for the wedding while being apart, I continued to prepare while he continued to serve. We just believed and moved forward.

Aaron returned from his mission in 1992. We believed in the power of the sacred sealing ordinance, so we wanted to start our marriage with those precious blessings to help us. Because no one in my family was a member of the Church, they could not attend the temple sealing. I was very close to my mom, as she had spent time as a single mother raising me and my sister. Unlike today, getting married outside the temple would mean having to wait one year to be sealed. I was heartbroken that she could not attend my temple wedding, but I felt impressed that we needed to start our marriage by being sealed. Aaron supported my difficult decision. We moved forward with that belief, and we were married in the Atlanta Georgia Temple about one month after Aaron returned.

After our honeymoon, we packed our belongings into a small trailer that we pulled with my two-door Nissan Sentra. Looking back, even the smallest trailer was probably too large for that little red car. But we believed we could make it from Nashville, Tennessee, to Provo, Utah, without any trouble. Many times, we drove up the mountains very slowly but came down quickly. I believe we had angels helping us with our load.

We arrived at our apartment in Provo and moved in. After paying deposits and buying food, we had three dollars left in our checking account. Because we came from families with modest means, they were largely unable to help us. We had to be self-reliant and find work. I remember both of us applying for several jobs and not getting any offers. Nothing was working.

One day, the pressure seemed particularly heavy as I had gotten another rejection. I knelt by my bed to offer a prayer to Heavenly Father. I pleaded with Him for help. I believed that all would work out, but that belief was waning. After some time on my knees, I remember feeling the thought, "Don't worry. Everything will be fine."

The next day I applied for another job, and a short time later I received an offer. We had set a budget for what we needed, and this job met that amount. Aaron likewise received some additional scholarship funding which would contribute to our finances.

When I look back, I see us as two naïve yet believing young adults. Our belief in Jesus and in the ordinances of the gospel pulled us through. Just believing was our strength. And that strength prepared us for even more difficult challenges we would face later in our family.

In this chapter, we will discuss the need to *just believe*. This simple yet powerful truth can help us progress on our faith journey. Belief is trust. It is acceptance. Fundamentally, belief does not require absolute evidence or proof. We *just believe*.

We have witnessed many who struggle on their faith journey simply because they stopped *believing*. They let go of *belief* to find *proof*. Searching is healthy. Truth is meant to be discovered. Evidence exists, and it can be found. However, knowledge gaps will always be present in spiritual things. At some point, we must simply *believe*.

If we are struggling with believing due to those gaps, we can accept Alma's invitation to begin with "the desire to believe." He said, "Even if ye can no more than *desire to believe*, let this desire work in you, even until you *can* believe."[271] Desire to believe until we can!

In what should we believe? King Benjamin gave us a list of fundamental things to believe:[272]

- Believe in God
- Believe that He created all things
- Believe that He has all wisdom
- Believe that He has all power
- Believe that we can't comprehend all He can
- Believe that we must repent, forsake our sins, and humble ourselves before God

The implications of believing these fundamentals are far-reaching. If we truly believed each of these things, so many of our doubts would subside.

Because of the spiritual power inherent in simply believing, Jesus similarly asked His disciples to just believe in Him when they sought for help and healing. He said, "Ye believe in God, believe also in me."[273] Below are examples from the New Testament of Jesus's calls to believe.

- To the blind men who sought healing for their vision, He asked, "*Believe ye* that I am able to do this?[274]
- To Jairus who needed healing for his daughter who had died, He admonished, "Be not afraid, *only believe*."[275]
- To the man who wanted healing for his son who had an unclean spirit, He said, "All things are possible to him that *believeth*."[276]
- To the nobleman, who wanted healing for his sick son, He said, "Except ye see signs and wonders, ye will not *believe*."[277]

In each case, Jesus simply asked them to *just believe.* This desire to have His disciples believe is most evident in the story of Lazarus.[278] Jesus had been informed that His dear friend Lazarus was sick. Despite the danger of returning to Judea, He decides to return and help His friend, whom He loved. Delayed on the way, Jesus informs His disciples that Lazarus had died. He then notes, "I am glad for your sakes I was not there, to the intent *that ye may believe*."[279]

When Jesus arrives, He meets a grieving Martha and later, a sorrowful and disgruntled Mary. Martha tells Him that His brother would not have died had He arrived earlier. She believed that He could heal the sick, but she did not yet believe He could raise the dead.[280] Recognizing her implicit doubt, Jesus tells her, "I am the resurrection and the life: he that *believeth in me*, though he were dead, yet shall he live. . . . *Believest thou this*?"[281] She replies, "Yea, Lord: I believe that thou art the Christ, the Son of God, which should come into the world."[282] Her belief was now growing.

After speaking with Mary, who also lamented that He had not arrived in time to heal her sick brother, they retire to a place where Lazarus had been laid for four days. When Jesus asks that the stone be removed, Martha reacts by saying that the grave would stink. Her belief was still too small. To this comment, Jesus gently asks, "Said I not unto thee, that, *if thou wouldest believe*, thou shouldest see the glory of God?"[283]

They roll back the stone, and Jesus calls with a loud voice for Lazarus to come forth. Miraculously, Lazarus emerges from the tomb! They unwrap him from his burial clothing and remove the napkin from his face, surely glorifying God. The record states, "*Then* many of the Jews which came to Mary, and had seen the things which Jesus did, *believed on him*."[284] Their belief had grown.

To progress on their journey of faith, these loyal disciples had to eliminate fear and doubt and just believe in Jesus. And when they did, He showed forth His power unto their convincing. Belief preceded the miracle.

We likewise must just believe on Jesus when the blessings or confirmation we seek have not yet happened. Jesus delayed His arrival so that His disciples would *increase* in their belief, not their doubt. We would suggest that the same is true in our day. We must simply believe, *then* we will see miracles occur. If we don't receive the blessing or answer we're seeking, perhaps the Lord is trying to develop a deeper belief in us. When we don't get what we want, we can believe He is preparing something far better.

To help develop the capability to just believe on Him, we will review seven belief-related invitations from the New Testament:

- Fear not
- Believe on His name
- Believe in the Light
- Believe His works
- Believe His words
- Pray, believing ye shall receive
- Help thou mine unbelief

FEAR NOT

The first important invitation about belief is that we must not fear. The miracle of raising Jairus's daughter from the dead best highlights the Lord's instruction on fear.

Jesus traveled to see the daughter (of Jairus) who lay severely ill. Unfortunately, she passed away while Jesus was in route—delayed while healing the woman with the issue of blood.[285] People informed Jairus of her passing, telling him to bother the Master no further. Imagine Jairus's pain and sorrow at hearing the tragic news of his daughter's death. Having no inkling that Jesus could remedy this fatal situation, Jairus must have been filled with fear. He was likely afraid of going home to his wife not having arrived in time with Jesus. He might have been afraid of what would happen to his family, and perhaps he was afraid of his own dark future.

Seeing this poor man's fear and sorrow at the loss of his precious daughter, Jesus lovingly commands him, "*Be not afraid, only believe.*"[286] Jairus had no idea what would happen next. Jesus took Peter, James, and John—who would be three apostolic witnesses of the grand miracle that was about to occur—and went to Jairus's house.

Upon arriving, Jesus was met by mourners who lamented the girl's passing. They laughed at Jesus's suggestion that she was only sleeping.[287] He dismissed the unbelievers, then took the girl by the hand and commanded her to arise. She woke and walked, astonishing all who were present.[288] Jesus calmed their fears and strengthened their belief.

Fear destroys belief. Many people falter on their journey of faith because of fear. Some fear that God is not real or that He is real but His love for them has not been sufficiently earned. Some fear that the Church they have believed in has betrayed them when historical facts they were unaware of are brought to light. Others fear that keeping the commandments means that they cannot have freedom. Some fear losing friends and family if they remain true to gospel ideals. Others fear losing eternal blessings if they remain true to social justice. Many fear losing loved ones to disease or losing themselves to despair. We have felt these fears in our lives.

To these dear, fearful people we say, *Belief in Jesus defeats fear.* For this reason, the angels at the empty tomb admonished the visitors, "Fear not ye: for I know that ye seek Jesus."[289] He is the great Equalizer, who will make all things right in the eternities. If we believe that He has all power to save and that His "grace is sufficient,"[290] then we should not fear but just believe on Him. To us, Jesus says, "Look to me in every thought; doubt not, fear not."[291]

BELIEVE ON HIS NAME

The second invitation is to believe on Jesus's name. The Apostle John invited us to believe on the *name* of Christ. Said he, "These [scriptures] are written, that ye might *believe that Jesus is the Christ*, the Son of God; and that *believing ye might have life through his name,*"[292] and "We should *believe on the name of Jesus Christ.*"[293]

What is the difference between believing on *Him* and believing on His *name*? All baptized disciples of Jesus Christ are asked to be His witnesses.[294] However, Apostles are special witnesses of the *name* of Christ.[295] Of this special calling and the meaning of the phrase the "name of Christ," Elder David A. Bednar taught:

> An Apostle is a missionary and a special witness of the name of Christ. The "name of Christ" refers to the totality of the Savior's mission, death, and resurrection—His authority, His doctrine, and His unique qualifications as the Son of God to be our Redeemer and our Savior. As special witnesses of the name of Christ, we bear testimony of the reality, divinity, and resurrection of Jesus Christ, His infinite and eternal Atonement, and His gospel.[296]

Therefore, Jesus's name represents all that He is and all that He did. His name is also equated to His power—the power to heal, comfort, enable, and, ultimately, save.[297] When we believe in His name, we trust and accept all these things. A firm belief in His name remains even when we face hard things such as doubt, difficulty, or distress, and that belief will help us move forward on our faith journey.

BELIEVE IN THE LIGHT

The third invitation is to believe in the Light. Jesus taught His disciples, "I am the light of the world,"[298] and He later admonished them, "While ye have light, *believe in the light.*"[299]

The Savior's first invitation is to believe in light while we have it. So many people do not fully take advantage of the light they currently have. They take for granted when believing is easy, when receiving answers is straightforward, and when salvation and love seem to be in their grasp. In their simplicity, they don't cherish and nurture their belief. Then, when the hard times come, they are less resilient and find difficulty in complexity and perplexity. We too have been guilty of this.

Jesus's invitation is to believe in the light. That Light is Jesus. We might suggest that Jesus's light involves divine truth, guidance and revelation, holiness and purity, life and salvation, and love.

Divine truth

Light and divine truth are synonymous. "Whatsoever is truth is light."[300] When we believe in Jesus we believe in *His* truth, not ours. Accepting the truths He laid out in His gospel will help us avoid the deceptions and the enticing "precepts of men [and women]."[301] Today's social media channels are filled with human precepts. Individuals with no expertise share their views, then others with similar views send these posts viral. Virality doesn't always validate truth. Believe in the light, not in what others say about the light.

Guidance and revelation

Light or enlightenment are associated with divine guidance and revelation. "I will impart unto you of my Spirit, which shall enlighten your mind."[302] When we feel that enlightenment to our minds—that spark of divine inspiration that leads us to do good—we should simply believe in that guidance.[303] And if we are in a situation where the light seems diminished, hearken back to previous times we were enlightened by His Spirit. Believing in the light of inspiration will keep us firmly on our journey of faith.

Holiness and purity

Light is often equated with righteousness, and darkness with sin.[304] When we believe in goodness, we will seek to be surrounded by it. We will begin to see goodness rather than weakness in others. Good begets good. Some struggle on their journey of faith because they lose the simple ability to see goodness in the Lord's Church and its leaders, policies, and practices. Believing the good—the light—eliminates the darkness.

Life and salvation

Jesus said, "He that followeth me shall not walk in darkness, but shall have the light of life."[305] Believing in the Light means believing in the mission of Jesus Christ to redeem all humankind. If we start believing that eternal salvation is not possible (or perhaps not necessary), we will falter on our journey of faith. Just believe that salvation is both necessary and possible through Jesus Christ.

Love

John the Beloved taught, "*God is light*, and in him is no darkness at all."[306] Later in the same letter, John teaches, "Let us love one another . . . for *God is love*."[307] What significant statements! God is light. God is also love. Based on these teachings, we would suggest that in the gospel of Jesus Christ, "light" and "love" are interchangeable. Therefore, accepting Jesus's light is to believe in His love for us, which He inwardly demonstrated in the garden of Gethsemane and outwardly demonstrated on the cross. A belief in this love will sustain us when we can no longer feel it in our distress.

BELIEVE THE WORKS

Jesus's fourth invitation is to believe on the works. On one occasion during Jesus's mortal ministry, He was in the temple teaching. Some listeners believed that He was divine, while others thought He was a madman or of the devil. With this controversy about His identity fresh on their minds, the people approached Him and asked, "How long dost thou make us to doubt? If thou be the Christ, tell us *plainly*. Jesus answered them, I told you, and ye believed not: *the works* that I do in my Father's name, *they bear witness of me*. . . . I and my Father are one."[308]

Immediately, the Jews took up stones to assault Jesus for blasphemy. To prove the Father was with Him, Jesus responded to their threats by saying, "If I do *not* the works of my Father, believe me *not*. But if I do, though ye believe not me, *believe the works*: that ye may know, and believe, that the Father is in me, and I in him."[309]

The principle that Jesus taught on this occasion is that we should believe His works. If they are good, He is good. If they are the Father's works, then the Father guides Him. The same is true for His disciples and His Church today. If their works are good, then they are good. If their works are Jesus's works, then Jesus is with them. Truly, "By their fruits ye shall know them."[310]

Believing Christ means believing the works of Christ. Any good thing leads to Jesus Christ.[311] All God's children receive the Light of

Christ when they are born. This Light prompts them to do good in the world. All who seek to rectify injustices, feed the hungry, clothe the naked, provide for the poor, and have compassion on the sick and afflicted are being led by the Light of Christ. Even those who do not believe in Jesus are prompted to do good because of Him.

Covenant disciples of Jesus have the added desire to be obedient to His gospel, which asks them to submit to the will of God, repent when they fall short, and endure to the end as faithful, obedient, and loyal followers. Observing the good that they do in the process of striving to comply with gospel principles should likewise grow our belief in Jesus.

Some struggle with believing that a person is led by God because unlike the perfect Savior, no person is either wholly good or wholly bad. Most people demonstrate a bit of both in their lives. Even faithful disciples sin. In the process of loving God, they sometimes fail to love their neighbor. They make honest mistakes. When we face doubts or distress, we can too easily see the bad in those who are supposed to be disciples of Christ, and we miss the great good that they do. Unfortunately, we tend to find what we are seeking.

If we have trouble believing, we should observe the works of those around us and look for the good.[312] When we just believe that Jesus is in the good that we see, we can increase our belief in Him. And we can increase our belief that He is with the people who do those good works. Most importantly, we can then likewise do His works. "He that believeth on me, the works that I do shall he [or she] do."[313] When His works become ours and we join with others in doing them, then our belief will grow.

Julie: A sister in our ward shared with us how seeing the goodness of the temple helped her family with her mother's terminal cancer diagnosis. We share her story here with permission.

> On March 2, 2023, I was with my parents as the oncologist delivered the heartbreaking news: Stage 4 angiosarcoma. We had three months left with our mom. Nothing can prepare you for this kind of news. But my mom, in her wisdom, knew exactly how we could process it. She asked me to take my dad to the temple that night.

> When I was in the temple, I felt a powerful impression from the Holy Ghost that gave me the comfort I knew my family needed: "When you want to be close to your mom, go to the temple." I shared this message from heaven with my dad as we reflected in the celestial room. This promise gave us the peace and strength we needed to face the days and years ahead.
>
> We knew our time left with Mom was limited, but we were given the blessing of time to gather all the family together before she passed. My parents had finished building their beautiful home just a year and a half earlier, directly across the street from the Pocatello Idaho Temple.
>
> When we gathered everyone together, we took all the grandchildren who were old enough to participate in temple baptisms to the Pocatello Temple with Mom. She was able to witness this sweet gathering of her grandchildren in the temple, fulfilling one of her dreams before she left this earth.
>
> The temple stands as a reminder of the sacred covenants we have made that bind us for eternity. Seeing the temple let us feel the peace and comfort of knowing a loving Father in Heaven and Savior were with us through this journey. Since my mom's passing, attending the temple has become an even more sacred experience for me. I truly feel God's love for me and can feel my mom close.
>
> I'm grateful for the temple and the power and strength it gives us by learning more about our Savior, Jesus Christ! I have learned to trust more fully in Him and to recognize His hand in my daily life. I know that because of His Atonement and Resurrection, we will see my mom again someday. Whenever we see the temple across the street from my mom's house, we are reminded of this sacred promise.

Seeing truly is believing.[314]

BELIEVE HIS WORDS

The fifth invitation is to believe Jesus's words. Jesus gave His disciples many precious promises during His earthly ministry. He promised them peace and comfort,[315] the Holy Spirit with His gifts and guidance,[316] answers to prayers,[317] strength and support,[318] forgiveness of and freedom from sins,[319] the power to overcome evil and darkness,[320] rest and relief from trials,[321] joy now and eternally,[322] and ultimately, eternal life with the Father.[323]

We often more easily believe these promises in our simplistic faith. However, when complexity or perplexity come down upon us, we may stop believing in these precious promises. We assert that the Lord will always honor His words. We must just believe them! We must believe even when we cannot see how or when they will come to pass. The Savior promised, "Whosoever believeth on my words, them will I visit."[324]

For any who may be struggling with just believing in these words of Christ—His precious promises—do not fear! We should not feel like we have disappointed anyone, including our Savior. Jesus taught, "If any man hear my words, and believe not, *I judge [or condemn] him not*: for I came *not to judge [or condemn*] the world, but to *save* the world."[325] In our view, the Savior is saying that He is patient with those who do not yet believe and does not rush to condemn them in their weakness. He came to *save* them and not *condemn* them. He is willing to help and most importantly, to wait as they find a way to believe His words.

If we wait patiently upon the Lord as He waits patiently on us to believe, we will see His words fulfilled in our lives. As Isaiah noted, "They that wait upon the Lord shall renew their strength; they shall mount up with wings as eagles; they shall run, and not be weary; and they shall walk, and not faint."[326] If we persist, we will eventually just believe in Jesus, and "If ye shall believe in Christ ye will believe in [His] words."[327]

Aaron: A dear friend and disciple of Jesus Christ received a terminal cancer diagnosis. His focus on the words of Jesus helped him and his family move forward in faith. I share his story here with his permission.

> As our testimonies of the gospel grow and develop, and as we learn line upon line, the depth and breadth of the gospel are unfolded to us in marvelous ways. But having noted

that, the simplicity of the gospel is what I love most about the teachings of the Savior, Jesus Christ. Whether it's a new convert to The Church of Jesus Christ of Latter-day Saints who is learning the first principles of the gospel for the first time, or the experienced member whose temple attendance has been consistent for years, the teaching is beautifully intertwined.

The first covenants of the temple endowment are obedience and sacrifice. I've recently realized that obedience and sacrifice are in many ways synonymous with faith and repentance. It's so beautifully simple: we find Christ, and then we make changes to come closer to Him. It was over the past year that I first considered the correlation of the things mentioned above.

I was given a terminal cancer diagnosis one year ago, not knowing how long my life may be prolonged. With no real warning of this news coming, it was initially a lot to process and consider. By force, perspective on life and death started to become clearer, the purpose of life evaluated at a greater level, and the things that matter most heavily weighed.

The first thing that our family spoke about was an evaluation of our faith in Jesus Christ and His gospel. This evaluation of faith, in many ways, is a question of whether we will let God prevail, or in other words, a willingness to be obedient to the things that He directs for our lives through personal inspiration and the commandments of His prophets on the earth.

The second thing that followed was an introspection of changes in focus or effort that needed to be made on my part to make the most of any time that may remain: Some things that needed to be corrected, and some things that were good which needed to be enhanced even more. The principles of faith and repentance accelerated in my life. So did my efforts to keep my covenants of obedience and sacrifice. But those things did not seem like separate and disjointed gospel living. They were one and the same,

> simultaneously allowing growth and progress in my personal spiritual sanctification.
>
> In the beginning, my cancer journey was about the cancer. As these things settled more and more on my heart, the journey became less and less about the cancer. I'm grateful for the miracles given to me and my health. I love the simplicity of the gospel, and it will be one of the things that I will remember most in going through this personal trial and experience. It brings such hope, peace, love, and joy amidst all we do, especially in challenging times![328]

My friend's belief in Jesus's words helped him accept his diagnosis and move forward as we can in our times of difficulty.

PRAY, BELIEVING YE SHALL RECEIVE

The sixth invitation relates to prayer. Jesus made the following connection between believing and prayer: "All things, whatsoever ye ask in prayer, *believing*, ye shall receive."[329] Just believing unlocks the power of prayer. However, this power may not always be the ability to get what we desire. Elder D. Todd Christofferson warned us, "We ought not to think of God's plan as a cosmic vending machine where we (1) select a desired blessing, (2) insert the required sum of good works, and (3) the order is promptly delivered."[330]

So if the purpose of prayer isn't always to get what we want, what is its purpose? Why believe in the power of prayer? Brad Wilcox offered a thoughtful insight. He told the story about his daughter who gave birth to a child that had an acute health crisis after delivery. He was at a women's conference when he found out, and he asked those attending to pray for the life of this child. He said that just because four thousand women were praying, that didn't guarantee a positive outcome for his grandchild. He then observed, "I don't think that prayers are what earn us blessings. I fully believe that God knows exactly what we need before we even ask. There's something that *connects* us to God and *connects* us to heaven as we pray, and it's in that relationship [that we find blessings]. That's where we start understanding why we pray. It's not to get what we want. *It's to build a relationship that's so personal and so strong, that we can trust God even when we don't get what we want.*"[331]

In the divine economy, belief in prayer connects us to God, and that connection will be a blessing that sustains us through the hard times that will always come.

To believe in prayer as a pathway to divine connection, we must believe in the pattern of prayer. Jesus taught us to pray.[332] Below is a summary of His teaching and our insights as to how that pattern can enhance our belief in and connection to Him.

Our Father
Address your Heavenly Father personally. Prayer is meant to be a very personal interaction and not just a transaction.

Who art in heaven
Praise and reverence His perfect character and attributes which define our eternal home. We express our belief in His goodness.

Hallowed be thy name
Give gratitude to Him for His mercy and loving kindness in your life, especially for His grace in leading you to this point. Thank him for specific acts of mercy, love, and kindness, not just for mercy in general.

Thy kingdom come
Express the hope for His great work of salvation and gathering to come upon all His children and your willingness to be an instrument in that effort. Cite ways you can engage in that work.

Thy will be done on earth as it is in heaven
Humbly state that you submit your will to His as do all the angels in heaven, noting specific ways you will act.

Forgive us our debts
Admit your weakness and your dependence upon Him, petitioning for His forgiveness and continued mercy through the power of the Savior and His Atonement.

As we forgive our debtors
Plead for the ability to have mercy on and forgive others—especially your enemies—offering them the same mercy you want from God.

Lead us not into temptation
Entreat Him for deliverance from external temptations and your internal mortal weaknesses.

Deliver us from evil
Implore Him for the strength to bear up and find deliverance from your problems, trials, and enemies. Plead for the meekness to control power and authority, the humility to control pride, and ultimately, the charity to overcome all.

Give us our daily bread
Ask for those things which you need and desire, always in accordance with His will.

For thine is the kingdom, and the power and the glory
Humbly recognize and express your faith in His wisdom, His power to deliver, and His kingdom, giving all glory back to Him for anything positive you receive, as did the Savior.

In the name of Jesus Christ
End in the name of Jesus Christ to bring forth the power of our Advocate who pleads our cause before the Father.

Believe in this perfect pattern of prayer. It will connect you to your Heavenly Father, and that relationship can sustain you when your hard times come.

HELP THOU MINE UNBELIEF!

The final invitation is a plea from the struggling believer: Help thou mine unbelief! Just believing on Jesus seems like such a simple principle, but we recognize the difficulty it presents to so many. When the stakes are high, the problems are complex, the outcome depends on others, trust has been betrayed, or the prognosis is grim, belief can be difficult. For some of the most heart-wrenching circumstances, belief can seem nearly impossible. We have felt that challenge in our lives, so we empathize with any who feel this way because of their own experiences.

A father in the New Testament felt this impossibility of belief due to his son's tragic condition.[333] He had brought his child—who was foaming at the mouth, cutting himself, and physically wasting away—to the Apostles to be healed, but they were unable to perform the miracle.

The father rushes to Jesus when He arrives on the scene and begs Him to heal the boy. When Jesus reaches him, the boy falls to the ground, writhing and foaming at the mouth. Asked how long this had been happening, the man replies that his son has been like this since he was a child.

Surely, the man, his wife, other children, and family had dealt with this tragic situation for an extended period. They saw no end in sight. Exhausted and heartbroken they came to the one Man whom they thought could finally help them. Desperate, the man pleads, "If thou canst do *any thing*, have compassion on us, and help us."[334] Any help was better than their current plight.

Jesus lovingly tells this man, "If thou canst *believe*, all things are possible to him that *believeth*."[335] The record of the man's response is among the most touching in all scripture. "And straightway the father of the child cried out, and said with tears, Lord, *I believe, help thou mine unbelief*."[336] With this last frantic plea, Jesus rebukes the spirit causing the condition, which "rent him sore" before finally coming out of him and leaving the boy seemingly dead. Despite getting worse for a moment, the Savior lifted the boy by the hand, and he arose. Finally, he *had* been healed.

This story follows the same pattern for any disciple of Christ who faces a seemingly impossible situation. After working and striving to find solutions—including coming to priesthood leaders with the authority to heal—sometimes there is no ready fix. We come to Heavenly Father in the name of Jesus in prayer and desperation because His Beloved Son is our last hope of healing. Yet, even with our pleas, the situation seems to get worse with no peace or resolution in sight.

Like this father, we may feel to say, "I believe, but help my unbelief!" What we are really saying is, "I want to believe, but this situation is so hard. I don't know if I can keep believing. I don't know if I can keep going. I've got nothing left. Please, help! Please, deliver me!"

To the struggling believer we say, "Hold on! Just keep believing. Don't give up on your Savior. He loves you too much. He will not leave you. He will lift you up in His time. The outcome may yet be unknown, and it may be different than you desire for reasons you do not now know and may never know. Whatever is meant to happen, just believe on Jesus, and peace will eventually return." We echo what the resurrected Lord told Thomas: "Be not faithless, but *believing*."[337]

Julie: We know a faithful Christian couple who went through a severe trial with their daughter due to her struggles with depression.[338] Always a bright, loving child, their daughter's personality seemed to change when she entered middle school. She began to be withdrawn and moody, and these negative mood swings gave way to angry outbursts and threats of self-harm.

Desperate, they took the girl to psychiatrists and therapists who attempted to help her to stabilize and cope with the depression and anxiety she was feeling. For an extended period, these clinical and therapeutic interventions seemed to do little to change the situation.

Sleepless nights full of worrying, watching, and praying for the life of their daughter led to fear, exhaustion, and desperation. They talked to clinical experts, counseled with ecclesiastical leaders, and prayed fervently to their Father in Heaven for His help. Yet, at their darkest moments, they chose to just believe.

Through much work, clinical treatments, therapy, love, and faith, this young woman gradually improved. This process was not linear for her. Improvement would sometimes stall, and she would at times regress. However, each cycle seemed to be better than the last, and eventually she arrived at a place of peace and stability.

The young woman became a young adult, graduated from high school, and eventually began working and attending college. She mentioned to her parents that she recognized the miracle of being alive to experience these life events. Her journey was an extended trial of belief overcoming fear in the face of very real, life-threatening danger.

Because the parents believed, their trust in Jesus grew. Because they believed, their love for their daughter expanded. Because they believed, their empathy for others' suffering enlarged. Because they *just believed*, their singular miracle has given way to more miracles as they have been able to help other families in similar situations. They have paid forward their belief to strengthen other struggling believers.

Belief on Jesus begets belief, which is perhaps the biggest miracle of all.

QUESTIONS TO CONSIDER

1. When have you believed in Jesus? How did that belief affect you? In what ways were you strengthened?
2. When have you struggled with your belief? What was the cause of your doubt? What could you do to just believe on Him?
3. What are your fears, and what is causing them? How could belief reduce them?
4. What words or works of the Savior could you just believe in right now? How could you build off that initial foundation?
5. How can you deepen your connection to God by having your prayers become a more personalized connection to Him?

NOTES AND INSIGHTS

6

ACT ON HIM IN FAITH

And [Jesus] said unto her, Daughter, be of good comfort: thy faith hath made thee whole; go in peace.

—LUKE 8:48

Julie: In July 2017, my daughter, Breanna, married her high school sweetheart in the Dallas Texas Temple. We spent much of the year getting ready for that special day. Because of the many tasks I needed to perform as the mother of the bride, I had deferred my annual mammogram until after their wedding.

In early August I went for my routine checkup. When the clinician was performing the test, she suddenly became quiet. She called others in to look at the scan. Following their discussion, they told me I would need to come back and have a more detailed image taken. They seemed concerned, and so was I.

My later scans revealed what we had feared—I had breast cancer. This news was shocking. I had no family history of this type of cancer, and I was only in my mid-forties. Although one in eight women will experience breast cancer, many women are much older than I was when they are diagnosed. This news took my breath away.

The doctor told me that I had stage 1 breast cancer, so mine was an early diagnosis. The mass appeared to be small and readily operable.

Later, I met with a breast specialist and received two options for the surgical intervention. I could have a lumpectomy where only the mass and a margin around it would be taken, or I could have a single mastectomy, a much more invasive operation. The choice was mine.

This decision weighed heavily on me. My original mammogram showed only a small mass, but a later MRI indicated that the mass could be larger. The less aggressive operation would mean a faster recovery but a higher risk of reoccurrence. The more aggressive option would mean a much longer recovery but a much lower chance of reoccurrence.

I thought deeply about my choice. I prayed earnestly for guidance. Aaron and I counseled together extensively. I felt impressed that I should go the most aggressive route and have a double mastectomy. Weighed by this decision, which I had to make in only one week, Aaron and I went for a walk on a trail near our house. I needed to talk it out. He listened to my reasoning and my feelings. He gave me his thoughts. He was not only my husband, but he was also my bishop. I valued his counsel; however, we both knew that the decision was mine alone.

Finally, I felt at peace with the path forward: I needed to follow the impression I had received and have a double mastectomy. This choice came to my mind again and again. I had faith that this was the Lord's will for me. When I told my breast surgeon, she was surprised, but she supported my decision. I did not know then why I needed to make this choice, but I moved forward in faith anyway.

My surgery lasted twelve hours, which included removal and initial reconstruction. Later, the surgeon told us what happened in the surgery. When she reached the mass, it was much larger than even the MRI scans had shown. I had a large stage 2 cancer. This advanced stage was not seen on the scan due to the unique nature of the mass. If I had chosen to do the less aggressive lumpectomy, the surgeon would have had to do a mastectomy anyway. I made the choice that the Lord knew I needed to make—even before the physicians knew.

I moved forward in faith on the Lord's inspiration, and He blessed me. I am now nearly eight years cancer-free. I have had three follow-up surgeries for reconstruction purposes, but there has been no reoccurring cancer. Faith truly preceded my miracle—as it can for anyone who moves forward in faith on Jesus.

In this chapter we will discuss the principle of acting on faith in Jesus. After we *just believe* as we discussed in the previous chapter, we must act on that belief to have it grow into faith. Faith is a core doctrine in the restored gospel of Jesus Christ. It's a core principle in nearly all religions.

According to the Bible Dictionary, "Faith is a principle of *action* and of *power*. . . . True faith always moves its possessor to some kind of physical and mental action."[339] James likewise stated, "Faith, if it hath not works, is dead, being alone. Yea, a man may say, Thou hast faith, and I have works: shew me thy faith without thy works, and *I will shew thee my faith by my works.*"[340] Therefore, faith is inseparable from action; if we have true faith, we *do* something with it.

Aaron: Once while making a visit to one of my ministering families, I shared a lesson taken from a First Presidency message by President Thomas S. Monson. In the message, President Monson provided a list of things a person could do to become an "example of the believers." One of the suggestions he gave was to "be an example in faith."[341]

While teaching this principle, I felt impressed to ask the simple question, "What is faith?" to the family's two children, who were eight and six years old. I expected to hear a Primary-appropriate response such as "Faith is believing in something," or "Faith is knowing that something is true." However, the answer I received from their six-year-old son was truly profound. He responded, "Faith is what you do."

This simple phrase by an insightful Primary-age boy caused me to ponder deeply the idea that the things we *do* are an expression of our faith. Perhaps, we don't always conscientiously connect faith with our actions, but these two things are interconnected—especially when unknowns remain.

Faith's essence is acting on imperfect or even missing information. "Faith is *not* to have a perfect knowledge of things; therefore if ye have faith ye *hope for things which are not seen*, which are true."[342] Faith extends belief by combining it with action when absolute proof is currently absent. Elder Joseph B. Wirthlin taught, "Faith exists when *absolute confidence in that which we cannot see* combines with action that is in absolute conformity to the will of our Heavenly Father. Without all three—absolute confidence; action; and absolute conformity [to the will of God]—all we have is a counterfeit; a weak and watered-down faith."[343]

The author of Hebrews makes the following statement: "Now *faith* is the substance [or assurance] of things hoped for, the evidence of things not seen."[344] What is the assurance or evidence of things hoped for? Faith! When we have faith, we act on a belief of things hoped for and things we cannot see. Those actions demonstrate confidence in those "hoped-for" things, and they are the evidence of those "not seen" things. Thus, faith *is* the assurance. Faith *is* the evidence. If we want assurances or evidence, we demonstrate *faith*.

Because faith and actions are synonymous, the evidence of a person's faith in a gospel principle is his or her compliance with it. For example, a person with faith in tithing pays it; a person with faith in the scriptures reads them; a person with faith in ministering serves others. And when our natural or fallen state results in sin or transgression, true disciples of Jesus exercise the action of "faith unto repentance"[345] to correct their standing with the Lord. Ultimately, everyone who has faith in Jesus Christ strives to become like Him.[346]

To be precise, the first principle of the gospel is *faith in the Lord Jesus Christ*,[347] not faith *alone*. For Christians, we must never disconnect the idea of faith from Jesus. Why? Jesus Christ is our Savior and Redeemer, the only Being with all power to mercifully comfort, heal, and save us. We can have faith in many things, but none of them can give us the assurance of joy now *and* life eternally.

Jesus gave us the strait and narrow path back to Heavenly Father. We must have faith in Him—which causes us to act on His words, follow His example, and strive to become like Him. Furthermore, we must do these things when we don't have all the answers, the path is obscured, or His presence is temporarily withdrawn.

Faith in Jesus Christ is simple but *not* easy. It requires fortitude in the face of fear, especially when we face complex, hurtful, or confusing situations. Complexity shakes our faith. Perplexity stretches the boundaries of faith, stressing it with an intensity that can be acute and sustained. We know because we have felt that pull ourselves.

When faith is waning, perhaps our first action should be to find ways to reconnect our faith with Jesus Christ. When we do, we will be better able to withstand the many and varied tests of that faith.

We would suggest five principles for increasing faith in Jesus: walk into the darkness, witness that ye are willing, experiment on the word, repent and forgive, and pursue small and simple things. We discuss each below.

WALK INTO THE DARKNESS

We must walk into the darkness to develop faith.[348] Why is this act of faith so important to God? Wouldn't it be easier for God to just openly illuminate to us the mysteries of the universe instead of allowing us to wander in darkness? Just handing us knowledge would be easier for Him, but this action would inhibit rather than encourage our growth.

Aaron: I am an adjunct professor to university graduate students, and I observe this process often with them. A student once told me that at the beginning of the semester she was completely confused. She had to look up terms I was using on the internet because she didn't understand them. However, slowly, through the course of my class, she learned more and more as she acted on what she was learning. The last day of class, when our teams read out their final projects, she finally saw everything come together. In that moment, she had an amazing epiphany and realized how much she had learned.

I believe our walk of faith with God is similar. He wants us to learn, so He doesn't give us all the information we need at the beginning of any life experience. He encourages us to move forward with partial knowledge and begin to act. As we do, we grow in our understanding and progress mentally, emotionally, and spiritually. We learn to trust Him; and more importantly, we love Him for trusting us to make the journey in the dark.

When we came to this earth to be tested and proven, we knew that part of mortality was to not be given all the answers. We knew that the Lord would give us guidance, but it would come "line upon line, precept upon precept; here a little and there a little."[349] We also understood that the Lord would only speak to us with a "still, small voice,"[350] one that is "a whisper."[351]

Why would a loving God not want to clearly, fully, and loudly give us direction on every matter we would encounter? Part of the answer lies in the principle of agency. Our Heavenly Father respects our agency so much that He is willing to allow us to make choices that might prevent us from coming back to Him. He has designed every interaction with His children with our agency in mind.

Because He will not direct every action for us out of His deep respect for our agency, we are required to have faith, a principle by which we act and move even when we do *not* have all the answers or *cannot* clearly see the road ahead. Thus, by its very nature, faith protects agency because it requires us to make decisions without full knowledge. Because we have many unguided choices to make, our faith is constantly being tested in mortality.

We sometimes hear people say, "I am having a crisis of faith." In this statement, we believe they are saying that the test of their faith has reached a crescendo, a maximum that seems almost too much to bear. We empathize with these dear disciples as we've felt similar crises.

To these individuals we say, "Find a place to feel gratitude for your difficult situation. The very moment you think faith is lost is when your faith in Jesus could emerge stronger than it has ever been." With this positive view of the trials of faith in mind, we might define faith as "grace under pressure."

The original Twelve Apostles had one of these defining moments of experiencing grace under pressure. Amid a terrible storm, they feared that their boat would capsize, and they would be lost. The Master was aboard, but He was sleeping. Like many of us in our times of trial, they felt abandoned.

Full of fear, they awoke Him, crying, "Master, *carest not that we perish*?" In other words, they, said, "Don't you care about us?" We then read, "And [Jesus] arose, and rebuked the wind, and said unto the sea, Peace be still. And the wind ceased, and there was a great calm."

"And he said unto them, Why are ye so fearful? *How is it that ye have no faith*?" Jesus's implied reply to their original question was, "Why did you think I did not love or care about you?"

"And they feared exceedingly, and said one to another, What manner of man is this, that even the wind and the sea obey him?"[352] The disciples stood in awe of His power over the elements but may have also wondered at His purposeful delay, implicitly asking, "If He had the power, what manner of men would wait to use it?" The answer: A perfectly loving Savior who cares more for who they can become than what it takes to get them there.

These disciples learned that fear quenches the fire of faith. They also learned that when the Master is with us, He can bring peace and stillness, even amidst the storms of life—if we will have faith in Him.

Elder Boyd K. Packer learned this same lesson when he was called as a full-time minister:

> Shortly after I was called as a general authority, I went to Elder Harold B. Lee for counsel. He listened very carefully to my problem and suggested that I see President David O. McKay. President McKay counseled me in the direction that I should go. I was very willing to be obedient but saw no way possible for me to do as he counseled me to do.
>
> I returned to Elder Lee and told him that I saw no way to move in the direction that I was counseled to go, and he said, "The trouble with you is you want to see the end from the beginning." I replied that I would like to see at least a step or two ahead. Then came the lesson of a lifetime: "You must learn to walk to the *edge of the light*, and then a *few steps into the darkness*. Then, the light will appear and show the way before you."
>
> He then quoted eighteen words from the Book of Mormon, "Dispute not because ye see not, for ye receive no witness until after the trial of your faith."[353] Those eighteen words from Moroni have been like a beacon of light to me.
>
> During the 29 years following that experience, I have learned over and over and over again that all of us must walk by faith near the edge of the light. . . . [Then] each of us must learn to take a few steps into the darkness of the unknown.[354]

Like the original Twelve Apostles and like Elder Packer, we must have sufficient faith to overcome our fear, walk to the edge of the light, and proceed a few steps into the darkness when we are confronted by unknowns, concerns, and troubles. When we do, our experience has been that the Light of Christ will illuminate the way we must go.

As Paul said, "For God hath not given us the spirit of fear; but of power, and of love, and of a sound mind."[355] May we move forward in faith and without fear, even at the darkest and most trying moments in our lives. Then peace will come, even if the storm does not subside how or when we would like.

WITNESS THAT YE ARE WILLING

Developing faith sufficient to walk into the darkness begins with willingness. Willingness is being "ready, eager, or prepared to do something."[356] Being willing is more than just a *desire* to believe; it is the *intent* to act in faith.

We covenant to be willing each week when we partake of the sacrament. The blessing on the bread states, "That they may . . . witness unto thee, O God, the Eternal Father, that they are *willing* [1] to take upon them the name of thy Son, and [2] always remember him and [3] keep his commandments which he has given them; that they may always have his Spirit to be with them."[357]

Notice that we witness that we are *willing* to keep these three promises. We do not covenant to perfectly *accomplish* them, only that we are ready, eager, and prepared to do so. When we *act* upon this willingness—however imperfectly—we unlock the Lord's promised blessings.

Why is willingness so very important in the economy of heaven? Willingness is an expression of our agency and a measure of our hearts. Outward actions follow inward intent. If our intents are good, then our actions will likely follow. Willingness is the "real intent" that shows the authenticity of our hearts.[358] President Russell M. Nelson gave this important insight about willingness:

> I learned that one of the Hebraic meanings of the word *Israel* is "let God prevail." Thus the very name of *Israel*

> refers to a person who is *willing* to let God prevail in his or her life. That concept stirs my soul!
>
> The word *willing* is crucial to this interpretation of *Israel*. We all have our agency. We can choose to be of Israel, or not. We can choose to let God prevail in our lives, or not. We can choose to let God be the most powerful influence in our lives, or not.[359]

Thus, willingness is a core trait of covenant Israel and is the motivating force for enabling God's will to prevail in our lives. In our experience, anyone who is not willing to act upon the things they learn makes little forward progress. However, people who are willing are blessed abundantly and make great progress on their faith journey.

EXPERIMENT ON THE WORD

Willingness is founded on a belief that what we are evaluating is good. How can we know for sure that something is good or of God? Alma gives us the answer with a proposed experiment.

In Alma's discourse on faith,[360] he describes an "experiment" of faith and invites us to try it.[361] If we have even a "desire to believe" or a "particle of faith," we can *do* a series of things to see if something is good. First, we will take the "seed" (in other words, a principle that we want to know about), "plant" it (embrace or live it),[362] and nourish it (nurture and care for it).[363]

As we complete these actions, we will see the seed sprout, grow, and "enlarge [our] soul"[364] if it is good. If the seed is not good, it will not grow, and we can cast it away.[365] Thus, the experiment for growing our faith in any principle is to believe it, live it, see the blessings stemming from compliance with it, and finally, gain a firm testimony of it. When we know something is good, we will be more willing to act on our belief.

The people listening to Alma asked him *how* to plant the seed or how they might exercise their faith.[366] Alma gave them an inspired response with the following steps:[367]

- Begin where you are[368]
- Search the scriptures[369]
- Worship God in prayer[370]

- Be grateful[371]
- Be sincere and authentic[372]
- Worship with the saints[373]
- Be humble[374]
- Be patient in afflictions[375]
- Sincerely seek Jesus[376]

These actions describe the process of planting—something that we can do repeatedly with any principle or teaching we are evaluating.

Alma then gave the people a case study in belief: the story of the brazen serpent.[377] In this story, the children of Israel were bitten by venomous serpents. To be healed, they had to gaze upon a brass serpent that Moses had lifted up. Many perished because they would not look. Why? "Because they did not believe it would heal them"[378] due to the "easiness of the way."[379] They were not willing to let God prevail because the experiment was too simple.

So what do we do if we struggle with our willingness to believe? Maybe we too think that Alma's experiment can't help us or that this process seems too simple. If this is the case, perhaps we can look to others we trust who have a firm belief, and we can trust in them.

The story is told of a little blind girl who was sitting on her father's lap in a crowded compartment on a train. A friend seated nearby said to the father, "Let me give you a little rest," and he reached over and took the little girl onto his lap.

A few moments later the father said to her, "Do you know who is holding you?"

"No," the little girl replied, "but *you* do."[380]

This simple tale is a story of faith, for the little girl who could not see had to trust in a father whom she knew could see.

When we *can't* see the path ahead, struggle with our willingness, or think that the process of building faith can't work for us, we should trust someone who *can* see, who is willing, and who is living a life of fervent Christian faith.

Having faith in another's testimony is a gift of the Spirit. The Lord taught us, "To some it is given by the Holy Ghost to know that Jesus Christ is the Son of God, and that he was crucified for the sins of the world. *To others it is given to believe on their words*, that they *also* might have eternal life if they continue faithful.[381] One gift is to have a testimony of Jesus, and another gift is to believe on the testimony of others.

We have come to realize that this second gift is not inferior to the first. Nowhere in holy scripture does the Lord condemn those who have the gift of believing on others. Perhaps this most important gift is available to some who have trouble knowing for themselves—now or perhaps, ever in this life. We would suggest that the Lord will celebrate and not condemn them for this type of testimony, which may be especially necessary during times of complexity or perplexity.

By leaning on the other person's testimony, those who struggle can continue their experiment. This action is an important type of faith—one that will sustain us even when we don't know for ourselves. It is a faith that we should not criticize but count on for support.

Julie: When Aaron and I were in college, our budget was tight. One day we got in our little two-door Nissan Sentra for me to take him to class, and our car would not come out of first gear. The automatic transmission had failed!

We took the car to a dealership for repairs, and we found out that the cost of the repairs was more than the car was worth. We didn't know what to do. The dealer showed us a good used car that we could purchase and explained that this would be a better option as this car was in much better condition than ours.

We went home to think about it and pray. Oddly, we felt good about buying the car, but we had no way to make the car payment. However, we were faithful tithe payers, and we knew that we had the Lord's promise that "windows of heaven"[382] would open if we were faithful. So, we decided to experiment on those words, and we moved forward.

The next day, I went to work at the dental office where I was the office manager. A few months earlier, we had lost an employee, and I had picked up her responsibilities. The dentist called me in that day and told me that he had decided not to replace this employee. Instead he would have me continue to do her responsibilities, and he would give me a raise. The raise was the exact amount of our new car payment.

We had experimented on the Lord's words, moved forward in faith, and the windows of heaven had opened. Our faith grew greatly that day, and this early experience with faith helped us make more difficult decisions in the future.

REPENT AND FORGIVE

Faith in Jesus naturally leads to repentance, the second principle of Jesus Christ's doctrine. Repentance is "a change of mind."[383] We change the way we think about ourselves; we change the way we think about the commandments; we change the way we think about other people; and we change the way we think about the Lord. We go from having thoughts of the "natural man"[384] to having the "mind of Christ."[385] When our thoughts have changed, then our actions will follow. Repentance causes us to become different—to become like Jesus.

Repentance is a critical act of faith because it is evidence of humility, a foundational trait of godliness. Change cannot happen if we are not humble; neither can willingness. If we are finding the desire to make changes in our lives—to believe more or to act in faith—these feelings are evidence of humility. Much good will come as we are humble.

Forgiveness of others also requires great faith. When we are hurt, abused, maligned, attacked, or harmed in any way, our natural protective instinct is either to fight back or run away. Neither response leads to forgiveness. The Lord admonished us to act in a higher way. "Of you it is required to forgive *all* [people]."[386]

Many times, the negative actions of others are the opposition that tests our faith—sometimes to breaking points. How much faster would our faith increase if we walked the path of forgiveness?

Jesus's disciples in the New Testament learned this truth when He taught them about offenders and victims.

> It is impossible but that offences will come: but woe unto him, through whom they come! It were better for him that a millstone were hanged about his neck, and he cast into the sea, than that he should offend one of these little ones.

> Take heed to yourselves: If thy brother trespass against thee, rebuke him; and *if he repent, forgive him*. And if he trespass against thee seven times in a day, and seven times in a day turn again to thee, saying, I repent; *thou shalt forgive him*.[387]

The disciples' response was likely what we would say: "Lord increase our faith!"[388]

Jesus explicitly warned them that they would be offended by someone. It is "impossible" *not* to be offended when the hurt comes. He did not justify the offender; He clearly stated that woes would come to that person. However, His instruction to forgive as many times as the offending person repents is truly remarkable and extremely difficult. If we strive to comply, our faith will certainly increase.

Thus, repentance and forgiveness increase our faith in Jesus. Without Him, neither repentance nor forgiveness are possible. With Him, all things are possible!

PURSUE SMALL AND SIMPLE THINGS

Once we decide to act in faith on Jesus, how do we continue to develop increased spiritual strength? We would submit that spiritual strength is developed and increased as we do the daily "small and simple"[389] things asked of us as disciples of Jesus Christ. These small and simple things include regular scripture study, prayer, expressions of gratitude, worship, Sabbath keeping, and service. Strength comes when we, like the Savior, simply go about "doing good"[390] every day of our lives.

More significant things will come as we pursue small and simple things. President Dallin H. Oaks taught the principle of doing small and simple things in a powerful way. He shared the observation that even a heavy cement sidewalk can be cracked by the small and almost imperceptible daily thrust from the root of a growing tree. He likened this to our own spiritual growth:

> So [likewise] is the powerful effect over time of the small and simple things we are taught in the scriptures and by living prophets. Consider the scripture study we've been taught to incorporate into our daily lives. Or consider the personal prayers and the kneeling family prayers that are

> regular practices for faithful Latter-day Saints. Consider attendance at seminary for youth or institute classes for young adults. Though each of these practices may seem to be small and simple, over time they result in powerful spiritual uplift and growth. This occurs because each of these small and simple things invites the companionship of the Holy Ghost, the Testifier who enlightens us and guides us into truth. . . .
>
> . . . [Other] "seemingly insignificant" private decisions include how we use our time, what we view on television and the internet, what we read, the art and music with which we surround ourselves at work and at home, what we seek for entertainment, and how we apply our commitment to be honest and truthful. Another seemingly small and simple thing is being civil and cheerful in our personal interactions. None of these desirable small and simple things will lift us to great things unless they are practiced consistently and continuously."[391]

If we sincerely want to develop a deep spiritual strength, we must begin by performing the "small and simple" acts of faithful Christlike discipleship every day of our lives. As we continue doing them, we will develop a powerful spiritual *thrust* that will enable us to carry out our Heavenly Father's work. In doing these things, we are not *earning* blessings or even salvation. We are acting in faith, which spiritually strengthens us slowly but surely. We will need that strength when the hard comes.

We should seek to simplify our lives, to slow down, and to stick to our eternal priorities, especially when we are faced with times of trial or difficulty. We are bombarded by so many good things to be involved in—sports, community activities, school events, and volunteer opportunities, just to name a few. Beyond all these good and useful things, the world offers us so many entertaining distractions—movies, TV, internet, social media, video games, leisurely pursuits, and an infinite number of other time-consuming activities—which may or may not be good, wholesome, or uplifting.

Each of these activities can take us away from those things which are most precious: our families, our faith in the Savior Jesus Christ, and our covenants with our Heavenly Father. Wholesome recreational activities are needful and are recommended for us and for our families.[392] However, when any one of these recreational items begins to dominate our lives, it can move beyond its intended usefulness and become a roadblock to our progress.

Elder Dieter F. Uchtdorf taught us this principle of simplifying, slowing down, and prioritizing when he said,

> It is good advice to slow down a little, steady the course, and focus on the essentials when experiencing adverse conditions. This is a simple but critical lesson to learn. . . . It's surprising how easy it is to ignore this lesson when it comes to applying these principles in our own daily lives.
>
> When stress levels rise, when distress appears, when tragedy strikes, too often we attempt to keep up the same frantic pace or even accelerate, thinking somehow that the more rushed our pace, the better off we will be. . . .
>
> We would do well to slow down a little, proceed at the optimum speed for our circumstances, focus on the significant, lift up our eyes, and truly see the things that matter most.[393]

Aaron: My parents are converts to the Church. My father joined the Church in 1968 at the age of nineteen. He was in the military, serving in the Air Force in California during the Vietnam War. Half a world away, my mother joined the Church in 1967 in Angeles City in the Philippines.

Shortly after his baptism, my father was transferred to the Philippines, where he met my mother at a young single adult activity. They courted and were married in 1969. A little over a year later, they were sealed in the Salt Lake Temple. I was born shortly thereafter: the first of three children. I have a natural-born brother and an adopted sister who is full-blooded Korean.

There was nothing particularly extraordinary in a temporal sense about my family. My father worked as an hourly manufacturing planner in the aviation industry, and my mother worked as a unit secretary at a hospital. At one time she worked two other part-time jobs to help make ends meet. We did not have a great deal financially when I was young, but my parents were honest and hardworking, and they provided for our needs.

From a spiritual and ecclesiastical standpoint, there was also nothing astonishing about my family. We were not descendants of pioneers. Other than the high council, my father never served in a high position in the Church. However, he and my mother served faithfully wherever they were called. They showed me by example the way to selflessly and consistently give of time and talents for the building of the Lord's kingdom. They taught me this principle as they served as temple workers in the Seattle Washington and Dallas Texas Temples for over thirty years.

In my youth, my parents made the effort to teach us gospel principles at home. We struggled like many families do with scripture reading, prayer, and family home evening. We made lots of mistakes. Notwithstanding, I remember many conversations I had with my parents related to gospel topics. These were not deep doctrinal dissertations or formal lessons, but they were consistent conversations where faith and truth were shared. Because of that training, my brother and I went on missions and were married in the temple. Those teaching moments blessed our lives immensely.

Although we have always felt very blessed, our family has also had our share of struggles and difficulties. When I was in college, my mother nearly died when she contracted pneumonia and then had an adverse reaction to medication she had been given. At the same time, my father was diagnosed with cancer and had to go through chemotherapy following surgery to remove the growth. Those were trying days for my family, but with faith in our Savior and with the help of good doctors and priesthood blessings, we made it through.

Yes, we've had both happy times and trying times in our family. Ups and downs have been a part of our everyday existence. However, the one constant through it all has always been our faith in Jesus Christ and our daily commitment to our covenants. With that sure foundation, we have been able to withstand all the difficulties and challenges we have faced, and I am convinced we'll be able to endure the many that surely lie ahead.

As you can see, there is nothing extraordinary about my family. We are far from perfect, but we moved forward in the process of perfection because of our faith in Jesus. I feel so blessed to count myself a member of the Bujnowski family. Much of the man I am today I owe to the righteous influence of my family.

I am sure my family is very much the same as many families—we are simply *normal.* However, out of that normalcy has come a quiet, peaceful faith in our Savior and a simple desire to continue to serve Him to the end. Although this achievement is not extraordinary as the world measures success, it is exceptional in terms of how our Heavenly Father views it.

And that simplicity will be what eventually saves us all.

QUESTIONS TO CONSIDER

1. What fears keep you from having greater faith in Jesus? How might you overcome them?
2. What situation are you now facing that requires you to walk into the darkness? What can you do to have the faith to take the first step?
3. How can you increase your willingness to act in faith on Jesus? What would that willingness look like for you?
4. How can you experiment on the word of God? In what ways can you test if something you want to believe is good?
5. What needs to change in your life to increase your faith? Who do you need to forgive to find peace? How can you muster the faith to forgive?
6. What are small and simple acts of faith that could help you grow closer to Jesus? What keeps you from doing them?

NOTES AND INSIGHTS

7

ALWAYS REMEMBER HIM

This shall ye always do . . . that ye may witness unto the Father that ye do always remember me. And if ye do always remember me ye shall have my Spirit to be with you.

—3 NEPHI 18:11

Aaron: Looking back on my life, I have precious, nostalgic memories that bring me warmth. Of all these significant events, I remember with a deep sense of sacredness the times when I received the ordinances of the gospel and made sacred covenants with my Heavenly Father. They pointed me to Jesus then, and their memory points me to Him now.

When I was eight years old, I was baptized a member of The Church of Jesus Christ of Latter-day Saints. My baptism occurred on the evening of my birthday, which was a Sunday. We held the service in an older building where the font was in the room we used for my Primary class on Sundays. My father performed the simple ordinances. He immersed me in water during my baptism. We dried off, and then we went into the chapel where he confirmed me and gave me the gift of the Holy Ghost. I remember feeling a peace I had never experienced. I remember feeling close to Jesus.

I received the Aaronic Priesthood and was ordained a deacon by my father when I was twelve years old. I remember being excited for my first duty: passing the sacrament. When the time came to serve, I put on my sharpest three-piece suit and with great dignity passed the sacrament to the congregation. I remember feeling like I was helping them remember Jesus.

After graduating from high school, I received the Melchizedek Priesthood. My father ordained me an elder. After the ordinance, I shook hands with all who stood in the circle. When I shook hands with the patriarch, a good friend of my father who gave me my patriarchal blessing, he looked intently into my eyes and said, "Congratulations, Elder Bujnowski." Surprisingly, those words hit me with force. I realized that I had a much weightier duty to represent Jesus as a Melchizedek Priesthood holder than I had as an Aaronic Priesthood holder.

Following my mission, Julie and I married in the Atlanta Georgia Temple. The ceremony was stunningly simple and tenderly intimate. I will never forget the feelings I had as we knelt across the sacred altar and made divine promises to each other and our Heavenly Father. For me, this ordinance was the culmination of what I had prepared for since my baptism: the end of a chain of sacred covenants. Simultaneously, it was the exciting beginning of something new: a new life and family. The weight of my responsibilities as a husband and future father did not yet fully sink in, but I had a sense that the journey ahead would be remarkable. I knew that Jesus would be with us if we were faithful to each other and Him.

In remembering these events from my life, one Person was central to all: Jesus Christ. When I remember the events, I remember Him. And His memory sustains me on my journey of faith.

In this chapter, we will discuss the importance of always remembering Jesus. Though it is a simple act, remembering is a powerful tool in developing faith in Him. When we believe and begin to act in faith on Him, we will experience a deepening of that faith as we consistently remember Him. Remembering unlocks greater blessings for us and keeps us progressing on our journey of faith.

Many who struggle on their journey of faith simply forget Jesus. They fail to remember the times when they felt His love; they discount the good feelings that accompanied positive spiritual experiences; or they intellectualize their faith in Him, trusting their mind more than their heart. We would suggest that remembering Him is a simple but powerful way to connect or reconnect with Jesus and amplify our faith. Remembering has worked for us in our difficulties, and we believe it will work for anyone.

Fortunately, covenant disciples have a regular opportunity to remember Him. Each week, we partake of the sacred sacrament ordinance. The bread and water are prepared, blessed, and passed to members of the congregation so they can renew their baptismal covenants. However, a covenantal *renewal* is not all that happens during this ordinance.

At the mission leadership seminar in June 2019, President Russell M. Nelson gave us additional insight into what occurs when we take the sacrament. He said, "Often, I hear the expression that we partake of the sacrament to *renew* covenants made at baptism. While that's true, it's much more than that. [When I take the sacrament], I've made a *new* covenant. You have made *new* covenants . . . in return for which He makes the statement that we will always have His Spirit to be with us. What a blessing!"[394]

As President Nelson taught, when we make our new covenant during the sacrament, the Father promises to always bless us with His Spirit. What do we promise in this sacred relationship?[395] The blessings on the bread and water contain our three promises, all of which are centered on the Savior, Jesus Christ. We promise to (1) take upon us the name of Jesus Christ, (2) always remember Him, and (3) keep His commandments. Only one of these three promises is contained in both prayers: The promise to "always remember Him."[396]

The repetition of this single phrase in both sacrament prayers suggests its high priority in our covenant relationship with Heavenly Father. The Father always wants us to put Jesus Christ at the center of our covenant discipleship. And how are we to focus on His Beloved Son? The Father implores us two times: "*Always remember Him!*"

THE IMPORTANCE OF REMEMBERING

Remembering is "to bring to one's mind an awareness of someone or something."[397] Why is the seemingly simple act of remembering Jesus so important for us as His disciples and as members of His Church? As we researched information on the power of remembering, we found two insights that helped us better understand why the Father would emphasize this aspect of our covenants as disciples of His Son.

First Dr. Eve Marder, a noted biologist, shared the following story about the importance of remembering:

> When I was young I had an outstanding memory. . . . [However], by the time I was a 4th year PhD student my memory was no longer as good as it was at 16. So, when I met Ted Bulloch, one of the greats in neuroscience, and I discovered that he seemed to remember every paper he had ever read, I asked how he did it. "You just have to *decide* to remember," he answered. I still remember how taken back I was by his statement. . . . I suspect that there is a deep message in what Ted said, and that we would all be better . . . if we *remembered to remember* more.[398]

As we "decide to remember" or "remember to remember," we will improve our recall. Remembering is a willing choice, and the more we do it, the better we become.

Second, researchers have tied remembering to the act of testifying. The authors of one study noted, "The ability to remember allows humans to distinguish knowledge about the past that they acquired *on the basis of their own experience* from that acquired in other ways.

"This ability constitutes the basis of testimony: An act of testimony is an account about the past that is claimed to be based *on first-hand experience. . . . Remembering . . . is the cognitive basis of testimony.*"[399]

Therefore, to *remember* Jesus Christ is to have *experienced* Him—personally and powerfully. In whatever way is customized in our lives, we experience His love, His redemption, His mercy, His deliverance, and His power. We will feel Him to our very core.

When we have these powerful personal experiences with our Savior, we can then *testify* of Him because the core of our testimony is not just what we *know*, but what we have *experienced*. Therefore, our agreement to "always remember Him" is the enabling action that allows us to "always testify of Him" because we have *experienced* Him.

We can only "stand as witnesses of [Jesus Christ] at all times and in all things, and in all places that [we] may be in"[400] if we always remember Him. Remembering enables us to powerfully testify how we have experienced the Savior.

Everything we do as His disciples is intended to help us remember Him. When we serve others, we should remember Him. When we pay our tithing we should remember Him. When we keep the word of wisdom, we should remember Him, and when we go to the temple, we should remember Him.[401] We should always remember Him!

Of the myriad things pertaining to Jesus Christ we *could* remember, three stand out as those we *should* remember: His plan, His loving-kindness and mercy, and His Sacrifice.

ALWAYS REMEMBER HIS PLAN

We discussed Heavenly Father's plan in detail in chapter 3 where we invited you to know and understand the plan. (We encourage you to recall it.) The Father's eternal purpose is unchanging: to bring to pass the immortality and eternal life of His children.[402] His plan enables His purpose; it is focused on our progression to become like Him.

The Savior's plan is the same as the Father's plan because Jesus has always done the will of the Father in all things.[403] The Savior's plan is designed to guard our moral agency and provide opportunities for us to grow and progress by experiencing "an opposition in all things,"[404] as we discussed in chapter 1.

His plan protects our agency by inviting us to make and keep sacred covenants with him. When we willingly choose to follow that covenant path, we forge a new relationship with God and with His Son. We connect ourselves to them in intimate ways—ways designed to bind us together eternally.

When we remember His plan—with our moral agency, life's opposing choices, and God's covenant path—we will be more likely to bear our contrasting experiences with an eternal perspective. We will not be confused or spiritually disoriented when we face difficulty, doubt, trial, or sorrow. We will develop faith in Jesus Christ as we experience Him in profound ways.

A friend of ours told us that when his children didn't want to do something that he knew would be good for them, he would tell them, "Trust me." Reluctantly, they would try the new experience.

Afterwards, they often realized that it *was* good for them. As an adult, one of his daughters got him a plaque that reads, "Trust me" with the signature "God" at the bottom.

We must remember to trust the plan and trust its Author and Finisher, Jesus Christ.[405] When we remember Him and His plan, we remember that "all things [in this life] will give [us] experience, and shall be for [our] good."[406] Remembering Him will give us peace amid pain, acceptance amid agony, and joy amid sorrow. It will provide purpose, even when His way is hard.

ALWAYS REMEMBER HIS LOVING-KINDNESS AND MERCY

Remembering His plan naturally leads us to remember our Savior's loving-kindness and mercy. As we mentioned in an earlier chapter, this plan has nine different names in the Book of Mormon. Among them are the *plan of deliverance*, *plan of redemption*, *plan of salvation*, *plan of restoration*, *plan of happiness*, and, significantly, *plan of mercy*.

Happiness, deliverance, redemption, salvation, and restoration are all acts of mercy. Mercy is the core of the plan, and it is a core attribute of the Savior. Without Him and His plan, we are subject to the full demands of justice. However, through repentance, His bountiful mercy is available to us.

Amulek taught, "Mercy can satisfy the demands of justice, and encircles them in the arms of safety, while he that exercises no faith unto repentance is exposed to the whole law of the demands of justice; therefore only unto him that has faith unto repentance is brought about the great and eternal plan of redemption."[407]

In this verse, mercy is treated as a proper noun. We might ask, who is Mercy? Jesus Christ is Mercy. He encircles us in His arms of safety. Of this mercy, we recently wrote,

> In the Old Testament, the Hebrew word often translated into English as "mercy" is *hesed*. More accurately, this word means "faithful and intimate, redemptive love." It could also be translated as "unfailing, faithful, steadfast, or loyal love." The word is "not merely an emotion or feeling but involves action on behalf of someone who is in need."

> Accordingly, when we speak of the "mercy" of Jesus Christ, it should bring into our minds His great act of Atonement, His unfailing actions to faithfully invite us to partake of His protection, and His loving-kindness in extending redemption, deliverance, healing, and strength to us despite our weaknesses.[408]

Jesus's mercy is manifested in His many acts of deliverance. Those who have received a mighty change or those who are preaching with the intent to generate a mighty change in others should always remember the Lord's deliverance in our lives.[409] Remembering His mercy connects us to Him and generates love; forgetting His mercy disconnects us from Him and elicits fear.

In the New Testament, we read of the Savior calming the storm. He was asleep on the boat while His disciples battled against the winds and waves. Afraid, they awoke him pleading, "Carest thou not that we perish?"[410]

Had they already forgotten His great love and mercy in healing the leper, casting out devils, and healing the centurion's servant? Unfortunately, they had forgotten. With great mercy and power, Jesus commanded the storm and them, "Peace be still."[411] Saddened by their fear and forgetfulness, He lamented, "O ye of little faith."[412]

When their trials were most intense, His disciples had not remembered His abundant mercy in previous deliverance. They had failed to remember that Jesus is full of grace and truth; and consequently, they struggled. We witness many struggling today because they have forgotten the great blessings they previously experienced on their journey of faith. We, too, have struggled when we have forgotten Him.

Fortunately, when we remember the Savior's loving-kindness and mercy, many positive things result. We move forward in faith, even amid unknowns, doubts or difficulties. Like Nephi, we will testify, "I know that [God] loveth his children; nevertheless, I do not know the meaning of all things."[413] Remembering His mercy unlocks abundant blessings through His infinite Atonement.

Aaron: My mother was born and raised in the Philippines. She grew up in a very poor family. Her family endured much hardship, especially during World War II when enemy soldiers occupied their country.

Her father and brothers had to flee to the mountains to hide from the danger while her mother and older sister stayed behind. One of eight siblings, she spent her days working in the rice fields and helping with other chores at the family home.

Mom joined The Church of Jesus Christ of Latter-day Saints as a young adult after she and her sister took the missionary discussions. She was excited for her new faith. She read the scriptures and learned the gospel in Sunday School lessons. She remembers seeing a picture of the Salt Lake Temple when she was taught about the blessings of eternal marriage.

She told me that she had hoped to be married in the Salt Lake Temple. As a new member, she prayed fervently each night for this blessing to happen, never realistically expecting it ever would. "How could a poor girl from the Philippines ever get to Salt Lake City?" she thought. However, the Lord mercifully heard her sincere prayers, and He answered them.

My mother met her future husband (my father) at a young single adult activity. He was stationed in the Philippines during the Vietnam conflict and had gone off base to attend Church. They were married by a Church of Jesus Christ chaplain after a period of courtship. Her marriage to my father, a United States citizen, allowed her to come to this country. A little over a year after they were married, my father and mother were sealed in the Salt Lake Temple. Her impossible dream had come true.

I've heard my mother say many times how thankful she is for the great mercy and love that the Lord showed her by allowing her to be married in the temple—not just *any* temple, but the Salt Lake Temple. When she faced other hardships later in life, she always remembered this great blessing He had given her. And that memory of His mercy sustained her faith and carried her through her hard times.

ALWAYS REMEMBER HIS SACRIFICE

Finally, with the Savior's plan and His mercy firmly rooted in our individual and collective memories, we will remember the act that made His mercy possible: His infinite and eternal sacrifice for us.

This most difficult of all journeys was required of Jesus by the Father, and Jesus accepted and completed it freely and willingly. There was no other way to offer salvation to the countless numbers of the Father's other children who would be forever lost to Him were it not for this selfless act of sacrifice by His most valiant child. The free and willing sacrifice of His perfect life was Jesus's precious gift of love to us. "Greater love hath no man than this, that a man lay down his life for his friends."[414]

Remembering His sacrifice is a primary purpose of the sacrament ordinance. We should remember that He suffered so that we might not face the same degree of suffering if we repent. The Savior taught,

> For behold, I, God, have suffered these things for all, that they might not suffer if they would repent; But if they would not repent they must suffer even as I; Which suffering caused myself, even God, the greatest of all, to tremble because of pain, and to bleed at every pore, and to suffer both body and spirit—and would that I might not drink the bitter cup, and shrink.[415]

As we remember His suffering and subsequent victory over death and sin, we will grow in our love and gratitude for Him. We will come to understand that through His atoning sacrifice, He will heal every wound, make right every wrong, and fix everything that is unfair in our life or in the lives of those we love. To us He implores,

> Listen to him who is the advocate with the Father, who is pleading your cause before him—Saying: Father, behold the sufferings and death of him who did no sin, in whom thou wast well pleased; behold the blood of thy Son which was shed, the blood of him whom thou gavest that thyself might be glorified; Wherefore, Father, spare these my brethren [and sisters] that believe on my name, that they may come unto me and have everlasting life.[416]

What love! What mercy! What sacrifice! What a marvel to remember!

BEWARE, LEST WE FORGET

The children of Israel were warned, "Beware lest thou forget the Lord."[417] Forgetting is easy, especially when times are good. We can take for granted good health, a stable job, a loving family, and close friendships. We can also fail to appreciate spiritual blessings like belief in God or faith in Jesus.

When we take lightly the blessings in our lives and do not recognize that their source is God, our faith diminishes. Why? Pride destroys faith. It overly focuses us on ourselves, our needs, and our accomplishments and causes us to forget any help we may have received from God and others. In our experience, no one accomplishes anything alone; we are all recipients of some measure of grace and assistance during life. When we believe that we are the primary or sole source of all the good and others are the source of all the bad that happens to us, we limit our spiritual and temporal progress.

Remembering increases gratitude, and gratitude fuels faith. Appreciation for God makes strong believers, just like expressing esteem for others creates strong relationships. We must take heed that we never forget the many people—including God—who have brought us to this point in our lives. When we remember, we grow in love and find more peace and satisfaction.

Ultimately, we must remember the infinite and eternal sacrifice of Jesus. Without Him, we would be eternally lost. With Him, we have the hope and promise of eternal life with our Heavenly Father.

Aaron. A few years ago, a friend of mine told me a touching story of remembering. Many years earlier, her mother was diagnosed with liver failure. She had never drunk alcohol, so the reason she contracted this condition was a mystery. She was dying, and there was no cure.

Fortunately, her life was saved by a liver transplant. A young man was tragically killed in an automobile accident, and his family made the difficult decision to donate his organs. Their sacrifice and his death preserved her mother's life.

In recounting the story, she spoke with great reverence for this young man and his family, even though this transplant occurred many years ago. Typically gregarious, she spoke in hushed tones when she told the story. When I noted that she spoke about the event as if it had occurred only recently even though it had occurred many years earlier, she remarked, "It is as real to me today as it was then. I will never forget what he did for our family."

Her comment touched me deeply. If she felt that strongly about someone who saved her mother's mortal life, should we not feel the same toward the One who saved our eternal lives?

Let us always remember Jesus Christ in every experience of our lives. In so doing, we will progress more rapidly on our journey of faith. We should:

- Remember Him, when we have doubts and questions
- Remember Him, when we receive blessings and good fortune
- Remember Him, when our hearts are breaking, and hope seems impossible to find
- Remember Him, when trials press down upon us, and our pain feels too hard to bear
- Simply, remember Him

May we always remember the Savior Jesus Christ—His plan, His loving-kindness and mercy, and His sacrifice and death for us. Always remembering Him is to always have faith in Him, despite life's calamities and unfairness. Ultimately, remembering Jesus Christ is experiencing Him. And experiencing Him only occurs by coming unto Him and following Him.

May we always *remember* Him. May we always *experience* Him. And may we always come unto Him and follow Him—whatever that means in our lives. For as we do, we will come to know Him, and He will come to know our hearts, for we will have given them to Him willingly and fully. As we lay everything on His altar, He will give us all He has, and we will become all He is.

His plan is merciful. He is merciful, and He is mighty to save and succor. May we remember Him when we are in our most desperate and doubtful hour and when we are at the height of our greatest triumph. For when we consistently remember to remember Him, He will consistently and personally succor us.

- In remembering Him, we will find hope
- In remembering Him, we will find consolation
- In remembering Him, we will find our Jesus

Julie. In 2020, the world shut down due to the COVID-19 pandemic. In June of that year, I began to have a fever that wouldn't subside. Several trips to the emergency room showed that I did not have Covid, but the physicians could not determine what was causing my high temperature, which spiked at well over 100 degrees Fahrenheit. They prescribed antibiotics, which didn't seem to work even after I finished them.

Worried after the fever lasted for eleven days, a family friend who is a physician had me admitted to a local hospital for more aggressive testing. He believed that I was going septic, and he wanted to intervene immediately. Due to the danger of Covid, they would not allow Aaron to come with me. They also put me on the Covid floor even though I had tested negative for the virus several times. I was very afraid to be on that floor, as I did not want to contract the virus.

Tests to find the cause of the infection were inconclusive. What was conclusive is that I was indeed going septic. After some consideration, the physicians believed a gall bladder issue was causing my fever, and they recommended that I have it removed. I had the surgery, my fever broke, and I was released to go home later that week. But that was not the end of my health issues.

After returning home, I had severe pain in my side. Attributing it to an issue with the surgery, my doctor readmitted me to the hospital. An X-ray in the emergency room confirmed that my diagnosis was hospital-acquired pneumonia, which had occurred during my gallbladder surgery.

After all my health challenges—my breast cancer with its associated interventions and then my gall bladder issue—I was flustered by this new unanticipated challenge. Why would this happen? Hadn't I suffered enough?

To get through my frustration, I had to remember all the blessings I had experienced in the past. I had to recall the miracles that occurred in the diagnosis of my cancer and the blessings I had received in my surgery and recovery. I had to focus on my faith in Jesus and His past mercies in my life to get through this new set of problems. When I remembered Him, peace returned.

My physicians were able treat my pneumonia. They discharged me, and I finally made a full recovery from my illnesses. I received an added blessing that I did not contract Covid despite being among many patients and caregivers who had been exposed. These new miracles were additional evidence that Jesus was watching over me.

Remembering Jesus brought me peace during this trial. Continuing to remember this and my other previous mercies from Him will bring me hope in any future difficulties I may face. Remembering brings us power. Remembering brings us back to Jesus.

QUESTIONS TO CONSIDER

1. What spiritual experiences in your life do you most remember? What made them so memorable? How did they point you to Jesus?
2. How can you think about Jesus more often in your life? What difference might that make with the challenges you now face?
3. When was Jesus's mercy most abundantly granted to you? How did you feel when you received these blessings?
4. How can you think about the Savior's sacrifice and Atonement more often in your life? How can you make your time during the sacrament more meaningful?

NOTES AND INSIGHTS

8
ENDURE IN FAITH ON HIS NAME

We know that all [people] must repent and believe on the name of Jesus Christ, and worship the Father in his name, and endure in faith on his name to the end, or they cannot be saved.

—DOCTRINE AND COVENANTS 20:29[418]

Julie: A faithful disciple of Jesus in our congregation shared with us a powerful story of faith and endurance from his life. He has spastic diplegic cerebral palsy, which causes him to have extreme stiffness in his legs that affects his ability to walk. I share his story with permission.

> When I was about four years old, I was admitted to Primary Children's Hospital in Salt Lake City for a major surgery on my legs. I remember the physician wheeling me back to the operating room in a little wagon. We passed a room full of bald children, whom I now know had terminal cancer. I tugged at the physician's pants and asked him what was wrong with the children. He told me that they were really,

really sick. I asked, "Are they going to die?" His response surprised me. "Probably. Probably they will," he said.

That response broke my little four-year-old heart. I didn't know how to respond. I remember watching them playing with their toys like life wasn't stopping for them. They were just playing like little kids do. That experience profoundly affected me. I realized that many of us are closer to death than we might think, and yet we can find some normalcy in life.

Ten years later, as a teenager, I had to return to the hospital for another major surgery. The femur had to be broken so the leg could be rotated into its proper position because my knee had become displaced as I had grown. A rod was then inserted to keep the leg in place. I awoke from the surgery in excruciating pain. It reached a peak on day five when the IV pain medications had worn off, and I could only take less aggressive medications.

The thigh bone was swollen, and they had nicked the sciatic nerve, so the pain was intense. I was sweating profusely and unable to get any relief because my leg was immobilized in a cast. My leg was throbbing; I had never felt pain like that in my life. I was also emotionally distressed from the years of struggling with my disability. Thoughts of, "Why did I deserve this?" and "What did I do wrong for this to happen?" filled my mind. I was angry at life, at God, and at everything.

In the middle of the night, I remember crying out loud to God, begging him for relief. "When will this end!" I cried. I never really knew how to pray until that moment. It was the most authentic prayer of my life, before or since. At first I thought God had forgotten me because nothing was happening.

Then suddenly, the image from my childhood of the children with cancer came into my mind. I had the feeling come to me, "Art thou greater than these?" It was like God was saying, "Look at these wonderful children that didn't even get to live as long as you have. What do you have

> to complain about?" My next thought was to ask for some kind of timeline for the end of my condition. The answer was, "Everything is going to be fine, but it's not right now."
>
> Those answers changed everything. If those kids could bear their pain and their fatal diagnoses, I could bear my current pain. And if God wasn't going to take away my cerebral palsy now or ever, everything would still be fine. The pain seemed to subside, and I made it through that difficult night.
>
> I think sometimes God wants to push us until we recognize that we really need Him. He was more interested in what I needed to become than in what needed to happen with my legs. And that realization has made all the difference in my life.[419]

This good brother is a faithful disciple of Christ and a talented musician. He grew up and earned a master's degree in piano performance from the Berklee School of Music. He blesses our congregation with his musical talents while still dealing with the disability of his legs. Jesus has used him to bless others despite his physical challenges because he has endured in faith on His name.

In this chapter we will discuss enduring in faith on Jesus's name. Jesus taught, "He [or she] that endureth to the end shall be saved."[420] Enduring to the end is a core principle of Jesus Christ's gospel. Our journey of faith lasts a lifetime, however long or short our time in mortality may be. Our lives are filled with ups and downs—contrasting experiences that enrich our lives but test our character. Some experiences (good and bad) last for an extended period. Our persistence in faith through these times and throughout our entire lives will be required for all disciples of Jesus.

Endurance is persistence despite trials or hardship. Continuing to the end of a present difficulty and the end of our lives can be challenging. Complexity or perplexity can challenge our efforts to remain on our journey of faith. However, failure to endure can cause us not to become all that our potential might allow.

Those who endure are resilient. Researchers at Harvard University's Center on the Developing Child studied resilience in children.[421] Their study highlights that a common set of factors that predisposes children to positive outcomes in the face of adversity. This includes the following actions: facilitating supportive adult-child relationships; building a sense of self-efficacy[422] and perceived control; providing opportunities to strengthen adaptive skills and self-regulatory capacities;[423] and mobilizing sources of faith, hope, and cultural traditions.

These principles hold true for adults. Resilient adults have supportive relationships, exhibit the belief that they can successfully perform specific tasks, develop adaptive and self-regulation skills, and use sources of faith and hope.

Organized religion with positive faith traditions can provide the infrastructure that meets all these requirements for both children and adults. In the Christian tradition, those with faith in Jesus Christ believe that "all things work together for good to them that love God, to them who are the called according to his purpose."424 Consistently acting on this belief in Jesus creates faith resilience."

We should not criticize those who are faltering in their endurance or resilience. We should help them! Perhaps, their lack of resilience is a cry for support, which is the primary factor listed above to having a resilient character. None are meant to walk the road of faith alone. We are to love, support, and carry one another through life's difficulties. Resilience requires support; it requires us.

We will discuss five aspects of enduring in faith on Jesus's name:

- Enduring well
- Overcoming by faith
- Finding joy in Jesus
- Having the permission to hope
- Holding all things together in Christ

These principles will help all of us endure in faith.

ENDURE IT WELL

The first principle of enduring is that we "endure it well."[425] Enduring well doesn't mean just getting through hard times. It means acting with grace and kindness and emerging from the other side of difficulty having become a better person. Enduring well is another example of "grace under pressure."

We recognize that good endurance is difficult, especially when the challenge is immense, or the attack is personal. Even more difficult is when we have been doing things in accordance with God's will and striving to treat others well, yet we still suffer. However, if we endure well in these unfair circumstances, how much greater will be our character! As Paul stated, "For what glory is it, if when ye are buffeted for your *faults* ye take it patiently, but if, when ye do *well* and suffer for it ye take it patiently, this is acceptable with God."[426]

Elder Neal A. Maxwell taught, "Our capacity to love and our capacity to endure well are inextricably bound together."[427] When we read the characteristics of charity, we can easily see why it's necessary to endure well: "Charity suffereth long, and is kind, and envieth not, and is not puffed up, seeketh not her own, is not easily provoked, thinketh no evil, and rejoiceth not in iniquity but rejoiceth in the truth, beareth all things, believeth all things, hopeth all things, endureth all things."[428]

Charity is a product of faith, which is another reason faith helps us emerge victorious from hard things. Elder Maxwell also insightfully taught,

> Whether, therefore, it is illness, pain, deprivation, being passed over, being ignored, being misunderstood, being underwhelmed, or working one's way through doubts, *trust and faith in our Heavenly Father and in His Son Jesus Christ and in His plan are what it is all about.* And we must have faith in His timing as well as in His existence.[429]

Julie: Two very good friends were strengthened by their faith in Jesus during a fiery trial in their life. He enabled them to endure it well. I share their story with permission.

In 2004, Tim and Kori Taggart were anticipating the birth of their fourth child and first son. The entire family was excited and anxious for his arrival. When Kori was about thirty-one weeks along, complications arose with the baby. While Tim was away on a business trip, she noticed that the baby was not moving. Concerned, she went to their local hospital in Tooele, Utah.

Kori called Tim to let him know what was happening. At first, she did not have a significant cause for concern. However, after the examination, the doctors decided to life-flight her to University Hospital in Salt Lake City. There was something seriously wrong with the baby. When Kori told Tim about the move, he immediately changed his plans so he could return home.

At the hospital, the doctors realized that the baby's kidneys were not functioning. After delivering the infant, the doctors' examination revealed that the baby had a rare form of leukemia. They began treatments which are usually effective. However, the disease had caused the kidneys to shut down, not allowing the medicine to properly pass through his little body.

Tim received updates of the baby's progress at each layover on his way back to Utah. Realizing the seriousness of the situation, he began to pray and ask the Lord to intervene in the life of his son. Amid his pleadings, he felt an unexplainable peace come over him which assured him that whatever the outcome, things would be okay. Because of Tim's delayed arrival, he asked his brother to give the infant both a blessing of health and a name and blessing. The baby was named Timothy Greg Taggart.

When Tim finally arrived at the hospital, he joined Kori, their daughters, and their immediate family, who had gathered to be with the baby. When all efforts to intervene had been exhausted, Tim and Kori made the heart-wrenching decision to allow nature to take its course. Dismissing the rest of the family, they remained alone with their son, holding him as he silently passed from this mortal life.

In the days and weeks that followed, their extreme sorrow at the passing of their little boy was lightened immeasurably by the peace and strength that they felt from the Holy Spirit. Although their family was not perfect, they had always strived to keep their covenants and to live the gospel. This sure foundation built on Jesus Christ enabled them to endure this trial without becoming bitter or resentful.

The Taggart family did not allow the passing of little Timothy to derail their discipleship. In many respects, it strengthened their family and allowed their faith in the Savior to grow. The Lord's grace has since flowed to them in countless ways as they were willing to put their faith and trust in Him. Because of their faith in Jesus, they have the assurance that they will hold little Timothy once again.[430]

OVERCOME BY FAITH

Overcoming is to succeed in dealing with a problem. We have witnessed many people overcome extremely hard things in their lives through their faith in Jesus. By acting on their belief in Him, they not only endured their challenge well, but they found success at the end of their long, hard road.

In the Doctrine and Covenants, we learn about the characteristics of those who enter the celestial kingdom—the place in eternity where God and Jesus dwell. In carefully reading the related verses, we only find four requirements. All other verses simply describe the characteristics of those who are eventually exalted and live with God and Jesus again.[431] The four requirements are: (1) they receive the testimony of Jesus,[432] (2) they live the doctrine of Christ,[433] (3) they overcome by faith, and[434] (4) they are sealed by the Holy Spirit of promise.[435]

The first three requirements depend on us and our faith in Jesus; the final is the approval by the Holy Ghost for our faith-filled efforts.[436] Having faith in Jesus and overcoming by that faith are both keys to our salvation. Overcoming by faith in Jesus doesn't always mean that things work out the way we *desire*. However, it means that because of our faith, things always work out for our *good*.[437] Through "endurance of faith on his name,"[438] we find peace, power, and purpose.

Julie: While serving as stake Relief Society president, I met a sister who suffered a most painful loss but who overcame her heartbreak through her faith in Jesus. I share this with her permission.

> Our precious, adventurous two-and-a-half-year-old little boy Luke passed away in an accident in March 2020. His passing occurred the week the United States shut down due to the COVID-19 pandemic. Schools were closed, grocery stores limited shopping, products were difficult to come by, and we were living our greatest nightmare. Only a few of our extended family were able to fly in to attend a funeral. Due to government pandemic mandates, we could only host ten people at the funeral service.
>
> Heartache. Pain. Grief. Fear. The world was in turmoil, as were our hearts. We yearned for peace. We longed for the

opportunity to be within the walls of the temple. We knew the comfort that comes simply from attending the temple. Unfortunately, for the safety of all, the temple doors were closed.

Several months passed before we were gifted the unique opportunity to attend the temple while a friend's son received his endowment in preparation for a mission. (During this time, only those receiving live ordinances and their guests could enter the temple.) Like a lighthouse in the midst of a foggy night, we were given guidance and direction that day.

We left the temple feeling an immense amount of love. In my journal that night, I wrote, "We felt peace, and our souls were flooded with love. God is so good and has an immeasurable amount of love for all His children." There was not a grand spiritual experience that day. I did not see my little boy in attendance. But I did feel an outpouring of love and comfort. The Spirit testified of the temple's goodness and the eternal truths taught there.

As time passed, the waves of grief continued, sometimes nearly overwhelming us. But as we kept our focus on eternal matters, we weathered the storms. The covenant of eternal marriage that my husband and I had made in the temple and our faith in Jesus Christ became the foundation of our hope. The sealing covenant bound our family together in those difficult first days, months, and years, both to those of us still here on earth and to Luke on the other side of the veil. Never before had those promises held such significance.

Eighteen months passed. Through a series of promptings and miracles, a premature baby girl was placed in our home. We felt our Luke close, guiding our family during this time. We felt his excitement for this development as well. In October 2022, we were given the privilege of adopting this precious child and being sealed to her. All six of our children, including Luke from the other side of the veil, joined us in the temple that day. We sat together with tears in our eyes, overwhelmed with peace.

> The Lord's ordinances are simple yet profound. The pain of trials does not leave, but with the Lord's help, we are more equipped to endure these trials with His sustaining love and strength. As we see His outpouring of love in our life we have come to understand more deeply His purposes and trust in His plan.[439]

Although this faithful mother and her family did not see the outcome they hoped for, they overcame grief, doubt, fear, and pain through their faith in Jesus and received a marvelous compensatory blessing. We too can overcome all through our faith in Jesus.

FIND JOY IN JESUS

In the New Testament we read, "We count them happy which endure."[440] A great paradox of life is that the joy that follows pain is sweeter.[441] Perhaps, the contrast enhances our awareness of the joy, or God blesses us with an extra measure of joy due to our efforts to just believe. Whatever the reason, we must push forward in the face of tragedy and hardship and look forward to the joy that will inevitably come. We reiterate what President Russell M. Nelson has taught:

> The joy we feel has little to do with the circumstances of our lives and everything to do with the focus of our lives. When the focus of our lives is on God's plan of salvation . . . and Jesus Christ and His gospel, we can feel joy regardless of what is happening—or not happening— in our lives. Joy comes from and because of Him. He is the source of all joy.[442]

Aaron: Some years ago, I served as a seminary teacher while Julie was serving as the Primary president of our ward. She presided over a good-sized Primary, with more than 120 children. A large Primary demands many teachers, and managing substitutes for those who could not be in class on any given Sunday was sometimes a full-time job.

Given that I did not have a Sunday calling, I became my wife's default substitute teacher to help her manage all the classes. Over the course of three years, I taught nearly every Primary class in our ward and spent a great deal of time in the nursery. I had a wonderful experience getting to know the children and watching as their budding faith grew each week.

Perhaps, my favorite group was the Sunbeams class. These energetic three- and four-year-olds were a delight to teach. Given their age and level of understanding, gospel principles were kept very simple and pure during the lesson. I learned to supplement teaching time with other activities, which included coloring, games, and stories.

Our favorite thing to do with the Sunbeams was to sing. We sang many of the usual Primary songs; however, their favorite song was—you guessed it—"Jesus Wants Me for a Sunbeam."[443] As others have probably also witnessed with Sunbeams, singing the chorus brought out a very special amount of energy and enthusiasm from these tiny disciples of the Master.

Each time the children said the word *sunbeam* in the chorus, they put an extra emphasis on the word *beam*, which included a jump with hands extended in the air: "a sun-BEAM, a sun-BEAM, Jesus wants me for a sun-BEAM. A sun-BEAM a sun-BEAM, I'll be a sun-BEAM for Him."[444]

I will never forget the smiles of delight on the faces of those sweet Primary children when they sang this song. Joy radiated from their countenances as they let their voices belt out the words. With their vibrant actions, they had become the very sunbeams of which they sang. They found joy in Jesus! And so can we.

Finding joy in Jesus comes as we endure in faith on Jesus's name. The psalmist taught us about enduring. He had suffered much due to his enemies, his children's choices, and his own sins. Yet he praised God and saw the endurance that can come through Him. He exclaimed, "His name shall endure for ever,"[445] "His mercy endureth for ever,"[446] "His righteousness endureth for ever,"[447] and His "dominion endureth throughout all generations."[448]

When we know that Jesus's name, mercy, righteousness, and dominion (or power) endures forever, we can more easily find joy in Him. We will have the confidence that He can help us endure because He endures. And that trust can give us the joy we seek.

PERMISSION TO HOPE

Hope is a natural outgrowth of faith.[449] It is a positive expectation about the future. As our trust and confidence in Jesus grow, so will our anticipation that things will work out or that a solution to our issues and challenges will be found. The saying is true: "Hope springs eternal."

In 1957, Dr. Curt Richter conducted a series of experiments at Johns Hopkins University that explored the psychological impact of *hope* on survival. He observed that wild rats, when placed in water, typically gave up swimming, and drowned within fifteen minutes. However, when Dr. Richter temporarily rescued the rats, dried them off, and returned them to the water, their behavior changed dramatically: they swam for as long as sixty hours.

Dr. Ritcher's experiment suggested that the act of being rescued instilled a sense of hope in the rats, giving them the endurance to persist far beyond their initial limits. He concluded that the presence of hope significantly affects resilience even in stressful and seemingly hopeless situations.[450]

We have seen so many people who lose hope when times are tough. The future is always murky and uncertain, but faith in Jesus gives us permission to hope. As Moroni taught, "Whoso *believeth in God* might with surety *hope* for a better world, yea, even a place at the right hand of God, which *hope cometh of faith*, maketh an anchor to the souls of men, which would make them sure and steadfast, always abounding in good works, being led to glorify God."[451]

Hope in Jesus is an anchor. It keeps us from drifting away and becoming lost. Because we believe He will save us, we can endure despite any desperate and seemingly impossible situations.

Aaron: Several years ago, I met an extraordinary family as I served as a member of the high council and as stake employment specialist. I share their story with their permission.

The father had lost his job at the peak of the deep recession that had gripped the US economy, and he had come to one of our stake networking meetings for help in his job search. Unknowingly, this event would only be the beginning of both the adversity and the miracles that he and his family would face over the next two years.

Despite his efforts to find work, the father remained without a full-time job for ten months. During that period, his oldest daughter submitted her missionary papers and received her call to the Argentina Buenos Aires South Mission. At about the same time, she began having repeated earaches. As a nurse in an ambulatory clinic, she received treatments for what they thought were ear infections. But when the earaches persisted, she was referred to a specialist for further testing to make sure she had a clean bill of health prior to leaving for her mission.

It was then that the first of this family's miracles occurred. The father was unexpectedly called back to full-time employment by his previous employer. Additionally, the health care laws had recently changed, which allowed their adult daughter to be included on their insurance. They did not know then how important these two events would become in their lives.

When their daughter went to the ENT specialist for her earaches, he did a detailed examination and found a lump on her thyroid. After performing a sonogram, he discovered three additional lumps. Initially, the physician did not have great concerns because these lumps can be common. But erring on the side of caution, he had a biopsy performed on the masses. To the family's horror, the tests came back positive: their daughter had thyroid cancer. She would require surgery to remove the masses.

With their daughter's departure for her mission less than one month away, they wanted to have the surgery as soon as possible. A successful procedure could mean their daughter might still be able to serve her mission. Unfortunately, the surgeon did not have any openings until well after their daughter's departure date. Upset, the mother related their dilemma to a family friend, who referred her to another surgeon.

With a trembling voice, the mother called the physician's office and related the urgency to the scheduling person. It was then that another of the miracles in this story occurred: the scheduler informed her that they had just had a cancellation, so the surgeon could see her daughter right away. Then, just before hanging up, the scheduler said, "I don't know why I am feeling so impressed to tell you this, but I want you to know that this is in God's hands, and we pray over all of our patients." What hope this message of love gave to this good family!

Following surgery, the family met with an endocrinologist to review the results of the biopsy and determine if the daughter could still go on her mission. He said he was willing to allow her to go and wait on her to return for her radiation treatments. She left his office to ponder the choice of postponing the treatment or delaying her mission. Although this decision was difficult, she felt strongly impressed that she should stay to receive treatments and leave on her mission later. At her farewell, she announced that she would postpone her mission.

Following radiation treatments and recovery, the young woman resubmitted her papers. Her mission was changed from a medical nursing mission in Argentina to a proselyting mission in Las Vegas Nevada, Spanish-speaking. Although her mother was disappointed in the change, this young sister accepted it with faith. Still wondering about that change, three more miracles of hope occurred that offered this family the assurance that the Lord was still watching out for them.

First, their daughter's companion at the missionary training center (MTC) was going to Argentina. During their MTC stay, they met with someone from the consulate for this sister's visa. While there, the consulate, out of the blue, informed them that there were a lot of problems in the medical community in Argentina at that time. The doctors were on strike, so people did not know from one day to the next if hospitals would be open. The girl realized it was a blessing to have avoided those troubles by choosing to delay her mission.

Second, Elder Richard G. Scott spoke to the missionaries in the MTC. In the middle of his talk, he said he felt impressed to tell the missionaries that things don't always go as planned and that occasionally, missionaries can put in their papers and then experience medical problems that cause a delay in their missions. After the medical clearance, the Twelve will pray about the assignment without looking at the medical release. He said that the missionaries should know that if a change in the call comes, it was as inspired as the first call. This knowledge gave the sister and her family a large degree of comfort.

Finally, when she arrived in Las Vegas, her mission president informed her that he had already made an appointment for her to see the best endocrinologist in the area. It turns out, this doctor was a former stake president, and he was willing to see her without charge (because he was not on her insurance).

During her treatments, the doctor sent her to a medical conference to be the subject of an ultrasound used to train the physicians. While there, she learned about another patient who had a similar cancer that had spread to the lymph nodes, requiring multiple surgeries. The sister realized that her own early diagnosis and treatment were a huge blessing, which gave her additional assurance and peace.

These experiences were tender mercies that assured her that the Savior was aware of her. Her name was known to Him. In fact, this young missionary's name was a reminder of the positive expectations she and all of us can and should have for the future. Her name was Sister Hope.[452]

IN HIM ALL THINGS HOLD TOGETHER

If, despite our best efforts, we feel overwhelmed and ready to give up, remember that we are never alone as we walk the path of discipleship. Our Savior and Friend, Jesus Christ, stands beside us to help and comfort us through His Holy Spirit. We must allow Him to bear our burdens, for He has infinite spiritual strength to offer.

Elder Neal A. Maxwell taught of Christ's important role as our great Rescuer: "When, collectively, brothers and sisters, things seem to fly apart for us at times, what fitting imagery [is provided by these words]: 'In him all things hold together'!"[453]

Faith in Jesus will be the binding influence that holds our lives together when they seem to be flying apart. When we hold on to Him, He will hold on to us.

Aaron: I served as a missionary in the Chile Concepción Mission. For a period of about six months (from 1990 to 1991), I served as the junior companion to the leader of the zone. Our area was Lirquen, a small town right on the coast.

While serving there, I met a man named of Brother Cortez. This aged man was the patriarch of a very faithful family in the ward. He was the first member baptized in this area—a Chilean pioneer. When he was younger, he would spend his evenings going out with the missionaries, walking the many hills of the area to teach the gospel with them. He was responsible for helping to convert many to the gospel of Jesus Christ.

Brother Cortez was unique not only because of his early conversion but also because he had been to the temple to receive his endowments and to be sealed to his family. Given the humble circumstances of the people and the long distance to the temple, many Chilean Saints had not been to the temple. However, this good man wanted to ensure that his family had the blessings of sacred temple ordinances, so he made the sacrifice to go.

We visited this family often, spending time talking about the gospel. I loved speaking with Brother Cortez. He was a faithful man who taught me a great deal about sharing the gospel and enduring in faith. We became friends. I saw him as my mentor and teacher, and I looked up to him for how he led his family in righteousness and how he endured faithful to his testimony of Jesus.

One day while my companion and I were walking in our area, a white truck came flying down the hill behind us and pulled up next to us. In the cab were Brother Cortez and his son. The son told us that his father had had a heart attack, and he was rushing him to the nearby hospital. He asked us to get in and come with them. We quickly jumped into the back of the truck and raced up the hill to the hospital.

When we arrived, we were hurried into the emergency area. Brother Cortez's son asked us to give Brother Cortez a blessing. I anointed, and my companion sealed the anointing and pronounced the blessing. During that blessing I had an interesting experience. I had the distinct impression that this good man would not recover and that his time in mortality was ending. I remember opening my eyes during the blessing and looking down at Brother Cortez—something I never had done before. His eyes were open, and he looked back at me. His look of fear changed to a look of serenity as the blessing promised him peace and comfort but not recovery.

Later that evening, the family called us to their home and asked what our impression was during the blessing. We both told them that we felt that he would not recover, and that his time on this earth was nearly complete. Although they were emotional, there was a beautiful sense of peace when we spoke. They had no bitterness or resentment that the blessing had not healed their father. They only expressed righteous resignation. They thanked us and began preparations for the funeral that evening. The next morning, Brother Cortez peacefully passed from this life.

My companion and I assisted this good family and ward leadership with preparations for the funeral. We were privileged to help dress the body in sacred temple clothing. We met with and gave words of comfort and counsel to family members. At the funeral service and the burial, I was asked to dedicate the grave, a precious priesthood privilege. Through it all, this family's faith in the gospel and in the priesthood remained strong and steadfast, even amid the sadness of their loss.

In 2024, Julie and I went to Chile for the temple marriage of our niece. While there, we went back to Lirquen, where we were able to have dinner with the Cortez family. After more than thirty years, they still endure in the faith of Jesus Christ. We reminisced about our special experience from three decades earlier, and we rejoiced that we were all still active believers in the Savior and His gospel. Despite challenges, their faith in Jesus remains. They can say with Paul, "I have fought a good fight, I have finished my course, I have kept the faith."[454] Truly, when things are flying apart, in Him all things hold together.

QUESTIONS TO CONSIDER

1. What situation are you now facing that requires you to "endure it well?" What does enduring well look like for you? What is keeping you from doing well in your efforts?
2. What can help you to overcome by faith in Jesus? How can you seek the support of others in your efforts to overcome?
3. How can you find joy in your current circumstances by focusing on Jesus? What brings you joy? Find a way to do those things in the coming weeks.
4. How can you increase your hope in Jesus? What can give you "permission to hope"?

NOTES AND INSIGHTS

9

MINISTER IN HIS LOVE

This is my commandment, That ye love one another, as I have loved you. Greater love hath no man than this, that a man lay down his life for his friends.

—JOHN 15:12–13

Julie: Before I went into the hospital for my first breast cancer surgery, I was very nervous. This procedure would be extensive, including removal of the cancer and the first round of reconstructive surgery. Two surgeons would be involved. Due to the extended time required, the doctors had explained that I would be put under a light general anesthetic for a spinal block. Then I would be given deeper anesthesia for the main surgery. The total estimated time would be over twelve hours. I received a priesthood blessing, and my immediate and extended family prayed fervently in faith for a positive outcome.

On the day of the surgery, after checking into the hospital and being prepared for the procedure, I was wheeled back for the spinal block. I vaguely remember coming out of the anesthesia and being in pain. Whimpering, I realized that I was still having the block administered. The only thing I remember is hearing my sweet nurse praying over me. Then, I fell asleep again.

When I awoke in my room after the extensive procedure, I was in severe pain. This discomfort continued some time without easing. I was also nauseous and unable to eat. This same ministering nurse was again with me. When she observed my difficulty, she immediately asked for some new medications, which quickly took care of the symptoms.

Throughout my stay, this same sweet nurse was my primary caregiver. She mentioned that she had a close loved one who had gone through breast cancer, and I believe this experience gave her greater empathy as she attended to my physical needs. She also administered to my spiritual needs. We had many conversations about faith and God, which gave me hope and comfort. When I was discharged, she personally wheeled me down to our car where she hugged me and told me that she would be praying for me.

My subsequent treatments included thirty-one rounds of radiation therapy. Angelic sisters in our ward took turns taking me to my many appointments. Often, I would sit in the locker room after a treatment, weeping from the pain. But when I would go out to the lobby, a sweet sister would be there waiting for me, ready to give me words of encouragement on the ride home.

Heavenly Father sent ministering angels in the form of my sweet nurse and those ministering sisters. I know they were sent by Him to make sure that I could get through this major trial in my life. How grateful I am for their love and compassion. They made a miserable experience tolerable and left a lasting impression on my heart.

In this chapter, we will discuss ministering in Jesus's love. As we move through our journey of faith—believing on Him, acting on faith in Him, and enduring in faith—we will begin to see the Light of Jesus Christ grow within us. As it does, we will want to reach out and share Jesus's love with others. Like the ministering nurse and sisters, loving our neighbors will keep them and us secure on our faith journey and prevent us from faltering. "He that loveth his brother abideth in the light, and there is none occasion of stumbling in him."[455]

As we said in an earlier chapter, light and love are usually interchangeable in the gospel of Jesus Christ. Jesus told His disciples, "Ye are the light [or love] of the world. . . . Let your light [or love] so shine before men, that they may see your good works, and glorify your Father which is in heaven."[456] Jesus loved everyone, so if we follow Him, we must love others as well. We will then become like Him: loving, kind, and full of charity.[457]

One of the sublime truths associated with our efforts to become like Jesus and develop Christlike attributes *for ourselves* is that those activities *turn us away from ourselves* and towards other people. This outward focus is the essence of service, and service is the essence of ministering.

When we minister, we seek to "succor the weak, lift up the hands that hang down, and strengthen the feeble knees."[458] We minister to others by delivering them—spiritually, emotionally, or physically—from the distressing situation in which they find themselves. We do whatever lies in our power to improve their lives. As we do, our own burdens become lighter, and our feeble knees are strengthened.

Jesus personally rescues us from death and from hell, offering us the hope of a glorious resurrection and eternal life with Him. He comforts us when we need solace through His Holy Spirit. He liberates us from the problems and difficulties of our lives, either by removing our obstacles or by giving us the strength to persevere through them. Many times, He sends His earthly ministers to assist in this effort. True Christ-centered discipleship encourages us to be His ministers by ministering to others. Spencer W. Kimball taught,

> We need to help those we seek to serve to know for themselves that God not only loves them, but he is ever mindful of them and of their needs. . . .
>
> . . . God does notice us, and he watches over us. But *it is usually through another person that he meets our needs.* Therefore, it is vital that we serve each other in the kingdom. The people of the Church need each other's strength, support, and leadership in a community of believers as an enclave of disciples. . . .
>
> . . . So often, our acts of service consist of simple encouragement or of giving mundane help with mundane tasks, but what glorious consequences can flow from mundane acts and from small but deliberate deeds![459]

Ministering begins by recognizing another's need. This action requires us to be attentive to any signals of distress. Sometimes we observe those signals through words or actions. Other times, the Spirit may whisper to us that someone needs our assistance. In either case, when those signals are received and recognized, we must act without delay. We must minister even if it means sacrificing our time, talents, or resources. Timely sacrifice is our "reasonable service."[460]

When we offer Christ-centered ministering to others, an interesting thing happens: We begin to see the Light, or love of Christ shining through us, which allows us to guide others in "paths of righteousness,"[461] and it strengthens us in our difficulties.

LOVE ONE ANOTHER AS I HAVE LOVED YOU

Jesus was once asked by a lawyer, "What is the great commandment in the law? Jesus replied, "Thou shalt love the Lord thy God with all thy heart, and with all thy soul, and with all thy mind. This is the first and great commandment. And the second is like unto it, Thou shalt love thy neighbour as thyself. On these two commandments hang *all* the law and the prophets."[462]

The Savior's response specifies *who* we must love: God and our neighbor. Jesus further clarified that our neighbor includes our enemies.[463] *Who* to love is unambiguous: we are to love everyone! As Dr. Adam Miller, a noted philosopher (and Church member) stated, "You have to use [gospel] law to judge *how* to love, but you must never ever use the law to decide *who* to love."[464]

Therefore, the important question for us is *how* to love God and our neighbor. In His final teaching to the Twelve Apostles at the Last Supper, Jesus taught them and us *how* to love. He said, "If ye love me [and my Father], keep my commandments."[465] He also soberingly taught, "This is my commandment, That ye love one another, *as I have loved you*. Greater love hath no man than this, that a man *lay down his life for his friends*."[466] Jesus spent much of His ministry showing us *how* to love God and our neighbor.

How did *He* love God? He was perfectly submissive and obedient to all His Father asked of Him. He said, "I seek not mine own will, but the will of the Father which hath sent me,"[467] and "Nevertheless not my will, but thine, be done."[468]

How did *He* love His neighbors? He served them. He listened to them. He healed them. He taught them. He cried with them. Ultimately, He gave His life for them. He did all these things for them—and us—because He *actually* loves us, not just because He was *commanded* to love us.

We would suggest that Jesus taught His disciples the two great commandments at the Last Supper because He was about to show them powerfully and persuasively for the final time in the Garden of Gethsemane and on the cross what loving God and neighbor really looked like. His sacrifice was the ultimate willing act of pure love. It was the model to show all Christians how to love.

We have wondered why Heavenly Father gave us the second great commandment when He could have just given us a single commandment (to obey Him). Then asking us to love our neighbor could have been one of His requirements. But He didn't. He gave us a second great commandment and told us it should be "like unto" the first, meaning it was just as important. Why?

We believe Heavenly Father is telling us, "I want you to love your neighbor because you *actually* love them, not because you are *supposed* to love them. I love them completely and authentically. I love them so much that I gave my precious, only Begotten Son for them. If you want to become like me, you must also genuinely love your neighbor. In fact, you'll need to love people who don't like you and work against you. I love people who complain to me and blame me for things. I even love people who don't believe in me and reject me. Can you do the same? If you can't, then you won't be able to live with me and share in my saving work for eternity."

Learning to love in the same way God loves us is our primary work as His children. By so doing, we will become more like Him.

BE AGENTS OF ATONEMENT

Despite our best efforts, we will all be broken, bound, or damaged to some painfully real extent in this life. We will be broken by sin, bound by habits, harrowed up by heartaches, distressed by relationships, shattered by losses, and dejected by disappointments. These events will push us into complexity or perplexity, threatening to interfere with our journey of faith. Ultimately, we will be defeated by death until the Resurrection, as all will have to pass through that final mortal experience and wait in the spirit world for the redemption of our mortal bodies.

So many needs, both seen and unseen, exist all around us, including in our own lives. Many individuals need our help. We can safely assume that everyone we know or meet faces some type of significant hardship. Some have a life-long physical, mental, or emotional challenge. Others have trials that are not as long lasting but are difficult nonetheless. A few struggle because of the agency or choice of another person, or they suffer simply because of a random, unfortunate event.

We understand that God "sendeth rain on the just *and* on the unjust,"[469] so no one is immune from trials and difficulties. Even people who seem to generally have it all together can face periods when they face setbacks and troubles. Painfully, we all may need help.

Although we are all broken in one way or another, Jesus Christ, through His Atonement, has the power to fix us. He can heal us and make us whole—physically, emotionally, and spiritually. Jesus is the great Renewer and Renovator of men and women. He is the only real way to receive comfort and healing in this life just as He is the only real way back to the Father in the next.

Jesus's deliverance and succor does not always mean that He prevents trouble from happening. He may strengthen us so we can "endure it well."[470] In this sense, He rescues us from pain by giving us perseverance and patience. He may save us from heartache by giving us hope. He may liberate us from loss and from loneliness by giving us love. Truly, we are "blessed in all things"[471] through Christ. Elder Dallin H. Oaks has taught, "The healing power of the Lord Jesus Christ—whether it removes our burdens or strengthens us to endure and live with them like the Apostle Paul—is available for *every* affliction in mortality."[472]

How do we then realize the marvelous healing power of Christ and His Atonement in this life, in the "here and now" when a soothing and comforting balm of Gilead[473] is so badly needed by ourselves and others? We would suggest that the answer is much simpler than we might realize.

The scriptures teach the sacred, and perhaps commonly overlooked, truth that "*all things* which have been given of God from the beginning of the world, unto man, *are the typifying of him.*"[474] This sublime passage implies that the effects of Jesus's Atonement can be seen in all the righteous things that we do in our everyday actions as His disciples.

As witnesses and disciples of Jesus Christ—individuals who have taken upon us His name via covenants and have faith in Him—*we* stand as His agents to bring the blessings of the Atonement to all Heavenly Father's children. When we realize that our righteous actions can be acts of atonement as His ministering representatives—actions of repair and renewal—we will develop a desire to minister to those around us. Fortunately, our own distress and doubt can be made lighter as we reach outward to help others.

A paradox of the gospel is that ministering in love to others helps to alleviate our own distress. If facing a crisis of faith, serve. If doubting our belief, give. If having pain and trouble, reach out to help another person whose burden is heavy. Ministering is the method of the Master to cure our own ills.

We can reach beyond ourselves to lift others up so that their burdens are lighter, and their problems do not overwhelm them. We cannot enable others to completely avoid the trials of life, however, we can walk with them in their difficulty. We can be equally yoked with those to whom we minister such that we share their pain and heartaches.

Day-by-day and person-by-person we, together with our Savior, can minister to *fix*, *repair*, or *rescue* each of our brothers and sisters in this life. Being "joint-heirs"[475] with Jesus implies that we are also "joint laborers" in His vineyard to bring atonement to others. We are agents and messengers on His errand of succor. As His ministers, He will often bless us with the peace we are seeking for ourselves.

Julie: Here is a true story—a parable of sorts—that illustrates the way our Savior sends His agents to help us after we have done "all we can do."[476]

When our two children were younger, our family attended a piano competition. We went to an auditorium near our home for their performances. Following the children's recital, we left the building and headed back to our car. As we crossed the road, I saw a small turtle making its way toward a wooded area across the street. After we got to our car, we sat and watched the little turtle move slowly toward the woods. We were concerned that it might be hit by a car, so we wanted to wait and make sure it was safe.

When the turtle finally arrived at the edge of the road, we saw that it could not get to the trees because of the curb which was too high for it to climb. We watched as it struggled to get over the curb, slipping back down again and again. After several minutes of this, I encouraged Aaron to go and give it a helping hand.

Aaron grabbed a napkin and walked over to it. When he got there, the turtle had its neck outstretched as far as it could go, trying with all its might to get over that curb. Aaron picked it up to put it onto the grass. Its little head darted into its shell, but as soon as it was back on the ground, it poked its head out and began slowly walking toward the woods once again. The turtle was safely on its way.

Each of us will have moments in our lives when we have reached our proverbial curbs—a barrier that seems so high or so difficult to overcome that we cannot do it alone. Try as we might—through our prioritizations, through our own spiritual strength, and through the wise use of our judgment—we may still have trouble moving forward.

This is the time that the Savior, in His tender mercy, will reach down to lift us up and help us do what we could not do for ourselves, often using others as His agents. This is the model of redemption. It is the model of atonement. It is the model of Jesus Christ.

Although the challenges we face are "common to man,"[477] we must, as Elder Maxwell encouraged, "respond uncommonly."[478] This uncommon response begins with our own efforts but generally ends with our dependence on the Man of Galilee who has infinite power to help and rescue us.

MINISTERING IS LOVE

How do we minister in love to others? The Savior taught, "Behold I am the light; I have set an example for you. . . . Therefore, hold up your light that it may shine unto the world. Behold *I* am the light which ye shall hold up—*that which ye have seen me do.*"[479]

What exactly did Jesus *do* during His earthly ministry? The scriptures are clear: He sacrificed His time and ultimately, His life. He served others every day of His mortal life. These acts are how He showed love.

There are myriad ways to minister—so many that we cannot list them all here. We might suggest that *what* we do doesn't matter, but *how quickly we do it* does. Elder Jose L. Alonso taught, "Each day we have the opportunity to give help and service—doing the right thing at the right time, without delay. . . . For many who have need of our help, it is not necessary to create new programs or take actions which are complicated or costly. They only need our determination to serve—to do the right thing at the right time, without delay."[480]

The word *atonement* means returning to a former state, returning home, being cleared of our spiritual debts, receiving protection from spiritual harm, and repairing that which was broken. We can pursue many ways to bring the Atonement's effects into others' lives through our ministering efforts. Here are a few salient but simple examples of how to share the love of Jesus through ministering:

- Follow the prompting to visit a brother or sister in need, someone who may need our comfort and counsel
- Invite a friend to a Church activity or a family home evening
- Put an arm around someone who looks low in spirit and tell them how much they are appreciated
- Search out family names then perform vicarious ordinances for deceased loved ones
- Give a priesthood blessing of health to a friend or a loved one who is ill
- Meet with someone struggling with his or her faith and just listen to their doubts
- Teach our children the first principles and ordinances of the gospel and be patient while they learn to apply them
- Learn from the scriptures then use that knowledge to teach another person a gospel principle

To be sure, the program of Christ's Atonement is a program of individual ministering. Our imperative is to find personal and loving ways to accomplish this work.

We are not alone in our efforts. The Savior helps, supports, empowers, and guides us as we love others. Ours is a beautiful relationship: Jesus is the Master, and we are His servants. We do our small part, and the Savior does the rest. Ministering is the practical work of Atonement. It lies in the acts of Christlike discipleship that we regularly carry out on our journey of faith.

In return for our efforts, we will find great blessings of peace and love ourselves. We can progress along our journey of faith and find our burdens lightened. To all who selflessly love others, President Thomas S. Monson said,

> God bless all who endeavor to be their brother's keeper, who give to ameliorate suffering, who strive with all that is good within them to make a better world. Have you noticed that such individuals have a brighter smile? Their footsteps are more certain. They have an aura about them of contentment and satisfaction . . . for one cannot participate in helping others without experiencing a rich blessing himself.[481]

Truly our light and our love will shine brightly as we give of ourselves and seek to quickly provide selfless service to those in need.

Aaron: While I served as bishop of a very large ward, our Valiant girls planned to visit a local hospital during the Christmas season. During that act of service, they had a very special experience that demonstrates the blessings that flow from ministering.[482] The leader of these girls shared their experience with me, and I share it here with her permission:

> The Valiant girls had been working for a couple of months preparing for this activity to visit the hospital and had been working hard making bookmarks, decorating folders, and making quilts to hand out to patients. Ours is a really wonderful group of girls, and they were honestly excited to know that what they were making would help and bring cheer to some pretty sick people. I don't think any of us knew just how much that would be true.
>
> On the night of the activity, in true Texas fashion, we had a pretty good storm with lots of wind and rain.

The traffic held us up and we arrived at the hospital about twenty-five minutes later than we had planned. The girls hopped out of the cars with their Santa hats on, ready to sing and spread Christmas cheer. Quite honestly, it was hard to contain their sweet ten- and eleven-year-old excitement! The volunteer coordinator met us in the lobby and immediately told us all to sit down and be as quiet as we could be. This was certainly not what the girls expected, but they were obedient and, although somewhat confused, sat in complete silence.

The coordinator left us there for a while. When she came back, she explained to us that there was a situation that needed her attention, so she might need to cut her time with us short. She then pointed out a young man standing at the check-in desk who we could tell was visibly upset. He was not yelling or being mean to the staff, but he was definitely in distress. She explained he had flown all night from the Middle East, where he was serving in the military and that they could not find the loved one he had come to see. They were not sure if she had been transferred to another hospital or exactly what had happened, but we could only imagine his stress over the situation.

At this point, the coordinator said she could leave him for just a bit and take us up to a few floors to sing a few carols and hand out the blankets we had made. We did this, and it was nice. It was what we had expected the night to be. Had the night ended there, the girls would have felt like they had performed a nice service project. But the Lord had another experience waiting for us.

Back down in the lobby, we somehow ended up with one remaining quilt that we had not handed out. We were about to leave when one of the girls told the volunteer coordinator that we still had this one quilt. She said there was a girl who had surgery recently, and she was still recovering in the hospital. She offered to give it to her. Then, one of our sweet girls said, "Can we give it to him?" and she pointed to the young military man still standing at the desk. The

> coordinator thought for a moment, and then said, "I think that would be wonderful."
>
> The girls walked over, and the coordinator explained that these girls were from The Church of Jesus Christ of Latter-day Saints, that they had made quilts for some of the patients in the hospital, and that they wanted his loved one to have one. At that moment, this big, strong, young man simply broke down. He turned around and began to cry. The remarkable thing was that he stopped looking at all the adults in the room. They had not been able to help him. When he turned back around, he looked at the girls. For the first time that night, he had some peace. There was a look of comfort on his face. The Spirit and those little girls brought that man comfort.
>
> The coordinator then asked us to sing one more song in the lobby. We sang "Silent Night." It brought new meaning to us all. "All is calm, All is bright." The Spirit was very strong that night. I know the girls felt it. We talked about it all the way home. It was a special night and one I will always remember.[483]

Of that sacred night, the volunteer coordinator later wrote in an email to our activity days leader:

> Your girls sang like angels during a storm. It was a very spiritual night. . . . It was just a moment in time. They made a difference in this young man's life. I honestly don't think he will ever forget his brief experience here that night. It had an impact on me as well. You see, my son is a soldier also overseas. May God bless you for all your help.[484]

We, like these sweet, faith-filled activity days girls, can be ministering angels in the storms of life that swirl around us. Ministering *is* love. When we express and give love, we become a little more like our Savior, and those who receive it will experience Jesus through us.[485]

SHARE OUR FAITH IN JESUS

As we serve and minister to others on our journey of faith, we will naturally want to share our growing faith in Jesus with them, spreading the Savior's light and love as broadly as possible. The Savior's final command to His twelve Apostles was "Go ye into all the world, and preach the gospel to every creature."[486] This divine injunction to share the truths of Jesus's gospel has been a hallmark effort of His disciples.

For sincere disciples of Jesus, sharing our faith is natural. Following Him is a way of life and not just a belief system. Our discipleship is manifest in the words we use, in the activities we participate in, and in the way we behave. As we live as followers of Jesus, our faith will be apparent to all who know us, so we naturally share it with others. As a good Christian friend of ours says, "You might be the only Jesus someone sees today."[487]

As with all ministering efforts, sharing our faith in Jesus Christ begins by loving others. Love leads to friendship, and friendship is based on mutual trust and respect. Friends spend time getting to know each other and learning to enjoy one another's company. When we make authentic friends, that relationship becomes the fertile seedbed into which seeds of faith can be planted.

Friendships are a positive starting point because we can share our faith in Jesus authentically when we have a relationship with others. When we have true friendships that are not grounded in an ulterior motive, but are grounded in heartfelt love and admiration, we can naturally talk about something as important as our faith in Jesus Christ and our knowledge of the restored gospel.

Friendships build trust and enable safe conversations. We can share our growing faith and trust the person with any doubts or fears we may have. Safety in our relationship will enable them to reciprocate by opening up about their faith journey. In the sacred space of friendship, the members can build upon the positive, address the negative, and assist each other in authentic spiritual searching. When people who are searching for Jesus act in this way, their combined spiritual power will be greater than the sum of their individual parts.

Whatever good things we are experiencing on our faith journey can be shared with others. I know a sister whose daughter struggles with her faith in Jesus and His restored gospel. However, she loves the music of the Church. So she listens to gospel music, and she sings when she comes to our meetings. Music is what she can share now to help her feel the love of Jesus in her life. And this is enough at this point on her journey.

Others may be able to share parts of their faith; for example, ordinances for their family, their children's participation in a Primary program, or another special spiritual event. Whatever the case, sharing faith increases it.

Julie: When our oldest child was baptized, we wanted to invite friends, neighbors, co-workers, teachers, and sports coaches to this very special event. We printed invitations that Aaron and I could give to people who had touched our lives in some way. When the RSVPs came in, nearly fifty people had accepted our invitation. We received permission from the bishop to hold a brief reception in the cultural hall of the building afterward.

The baptismal and confirmation ordinances were uplifting. Our guests were touched by the closing song, "I'm Trying to Be Like Jesus." At the reception our friends enjoyed the fellowship of our ward members. Given that we lived in a relatively small town in Texas, many already knew at least one person there. This event made such an impact on a few people, that afterward, Aaron and I had several discussions with them about faith and belief.

We followed this same pattern with the baby blessing for our youngest. This time, we had six or seven friends who gladly accepted the invitation to attend the meeting. This date was also the day of the Primary program, which ended up being a very special experience for our guests.

Because of our authentic relationship with these good-hearted people, inviting them to the baptism and the baby blessing was very easy. We loved, we shared, then we invited them to join us on a part of our faith journey. Their faith in Jesus grew as did ours.

Each of us can have similar interactions with our friends as we authentically love, share and invite. If we develop true friendships with others, we can easily and naturally find various ways to share our faith and our love of Jesus with them. Our interactions will be as the words of the prophet Isaiah: "Come ye, and let us walk [together] in the light of the Lord."[488]

Faith grows when it is shared, just as doubts increase when they are shared. May we share our faith—in whatever stage or state it may be—so we may grow together with those whom we love.

CONTINUE YE IN MY LOVE

Jesus invited His disciples, "Continue ye in my love."[489] Persistent ministering to others can be difficult when we don't feel the love of God in our lives. Difficulty has a way of hardening tender hearts. However, we would encourage you to "press forward with a steadfastness in Christ, having a perfect brightness of hope, and a *love of God and of all [people]*."[490] In previous chapters, we encouraged you to just believe, and just have faith. We now make this invitation: *Just love*!

We can start with small acts of goodness for those closest to us and easiest to love. As we build on those experiences, our ability to love will increase and our radius of love will expand. Love given will be love received when others appreciate our kindness. When we feel our love reciprocated, we can consider that God is delivering His love to *us*, just as we were the means of giving it to others. Reciprocated love is God's love, and it will sustain us on our journey of faith.

QUESTIONS TO CONSIDER

1. How can you be more attentive to the physical, emotional, and spiritual needs of those around you?
2. How could ministering to others' needs help you with your own difficulties? Why does service lift us up?
3. When others minister to you, how do you feel? How can you convey your gratitude to those who minister to you?
4. Think of someone you know who is struggling. How can you show them love? When will you plan to do this?
5. How can you create a safe space for your friends to share their faith *and* their doubts? How can you listen with greater empathy and kindness?

NOTES AND INSIGHTS

10

WITNESS A MIGHTY CHANGE

We believe all the words which thou hast spoken unto us; and also, we know of their surety and truth, because of the Spirit of the Lord Omnipotent, which has wrought a mighty change in us, or in our hearts."

—MOSIAH 5:2

Aaron: In 2024, Julie and I went to Concepción, Chile (where I served my mission), to attend our niece's wedding and temple sealing to a young Chilean man. While there, we went to visit some families I had known during my mission over thirty years earlier. One experience touched me deeply.

We visited the house of a sister named Lorena. Lorena was a young single adult during the years of my mission. She lived next door to a couple who provided housing to the missionaries. The first set of missionaries who taught Lorena were sisters who were temporarily in the area on an exchange. Her mother accidentally told her that some friends were looking for her, and those friends turned out to be the sister missionaries. After that first talk with them, Lorena took the discussions off and on with various missionaries for a while.

Eventually, I arrived in the area as the junior companion to a zone leader. We lived with the couple next door to Lorena. They suggested that we teach her again. I remember going next door and introducing myself. When we asked if she would receive our lessons, she agreed. This time, something was different. She was more receptive than before, and she decided to act on her faith in Jesus and agreed to follow Him by being baptized.

I was transferred shortly afterward, and I didn't see her again until Julie and I went to her home—the same home where I taught her the first time—over thirty years later. She was so happy to see me. She said that I was "her missionary." When we started to talk, I asked her why she finally decided to be baptized those many years ago. She said that she just knew it was time. Her heart had changed.

In the years that have passed, many positive things happened in her life due to that mighty change of heart. Lorena married in the temple. She served as a stake Primary president, and she had been teaching seminary for eight years. Her husband was the last branch president and the first bishop of their ward. He subsequently served as bishop twice, then in the stake presidency for nine years. He was serving as the elders quorum president at the time of our visit. We met Lorena's two young adult sons. They are both returned missionaries and are firm in the faith of Jesus.

We talked about how the gospel of Jesus Christ had changed our lives and made us better. It was clear that her faith in Him had made the difference. Lorena does cross-stitch, and she gifted Julie a beautiful stitching. Julie gave her a huge hug and thanked her. Meeting with her was a highlight of our trip to Chile.

Lorena's mighty change of heart altered the course of her life. A simple decision to follow Jesus led to many other precious blessings for her and many others. A changed heart touches other hearts, which is the power of conversion. It is the power of Jesus.

In this chapter we will discuss witnessing a mighty change in our hearts. When we have followed God's pattern of faith—experiencing an opposition, knowing God's plan of mercy, seeking this Jesus, just believing on Him, acting on faith in Him, always remembering Him, enduring in faith on His name, and ministering in His love—we are prepared to experience a "mighty change" in our hearts.

In our experience, a mighty change is made up of many mini changes—spiritual inflection points that slowly and consistently move us toward Jesus. The change becomes "mighty" in us or in our hearts when we have "no more disposition [or desire] to do evil, but to do good [and follow Jesus] continually."[491] And even then, this mighty change doesn't mean we *won't* do something wrong—just that we won't *desire* to do it. Following the challenges of *complexity* and *perplexity*, our mighty change brings us *harmony* on our journey of faith.

Harmony does *not* mean that we have *all* the answers or that *all* our issues are resolved. It means that not having all the answers and not having all our issues resolved no longer confounds us. We find peace despite our gaps in understanding. We find faith. We are born again in Jesus.

The prophet Alma asked these penetrating questions to his people: "Have ye spiritually been born of God? Have ye received his image in your countenances? Have ye experienced this *mighty change* in your hearts?"[492] In his words, a mighty change is to be born again of God. It is to have become like Him in the very way we look, think, and act. A mighty change is full conversion to Jesus. It is harmony.

We would suggest that full conversion to Jesus is synonymous with full commitment to Him and His gospel. Elder D. Todd Christofferson taught that we are fully converted when we "make the gospel of Jesus Christ not just an *influence* in [our lives] but the *controlling influence* and, indeed, the very core of what [we] are."[493] Full commitment means we are "all in," which gives us spiritual protection from falling away from Jesus.[494]

Being "all in" makes us "but if not" disciples of Jesus. In the Old Testament, Shadrach, Meshack, and Abednego were going to be thrown into a fiery furnace for living their beliefs which were against the law of the land. When the king asked them if their God would deliver them, they responded that they believed He would. Then, they resolutely said, "*But if not* [meaning if He doesn't save us] . . . we will not serve thy gods."[495] Disciples with a mighty change of heart are committed despite any consequence they might face. They find harmony even amid tragedy.

Committing to Jesus and changing means leaving behind our biases and preferences and adopting those of Jesus. We jettison our views and adopt His perspectives. We make our preferences equal to His desires. We no longer worry about what we don't know; we concentrate on what we know through Him. These modifications are "mighty" because change is hard. Humans do not like change. For most people, change happens slowly and over time but only if we want it to happen.

Elder Christofferson also taught, "For most of us, the changes [to become converted to Jesus] are more gradual and occur over time. Being born again, unlike our physical birth, is more a *process* than an *event*. And engaging in that process is the central purpose of mortality."[496]

Mightiness doesn't describe the *end* of the change but the challenge in its *process*. Change is conversion. And conversion is being born again a "new creature" in Christ, where old habits, desires, and actions have passed away and all things have become new and found harmony.[497] We will discuss four concepts related to our mighty change:

- Being converted unto the Lord
- Finding power in Him
- Becoming like Him
- Becoming perfect, eventually

CONVERTED UNTO THE LORD

What does it mean to "be converted"? Elder Richard G. Scott shared the following insight.

> *Converted* means to turn from one belief or course of action to another. Conversion is a spiritual and moral change. Converted implies not merely mental acceptance of Jesus and his teachings but also a motivating faith in him and His gospel. A faith which works a transformation, an actual change in one's understanding of life's meaning and in his allegiance to God in interest, in thought, and in conduct.[498]

Conversion is change, and full conversion is a mighty change. We want to note that we are converted to *Jesus*, not to His Church. *He* is the One in whom we have faith; *He* is the One who has all power to save; *He* is the One whom we love, and the One who loves us. Of being converted unto the Lord and *not* the Church, Elder D. Todd

Christofferson emphasized, "We do *not* strive for conversion to the *Church* but to *Christ* and His gospel, a conversion that is *facilitated by* the Church. The Book of Mormon expresses it best when it says that the people "were converted unto the Lord, and were united unto the church of Christ.""[499]

The Church is the vehicle for guiding us to Christ. Jesus is *perfect.* Through an ongoing restoration, the Church is *being perfected* by Him. When we have faith in Jesus, we can be patient with the process of perfection in His Church, just as He was with His imperfect Apostles who led the early Christian church.

We walk the path to conversion when we have faith in Jesus, learn His gospel, and gain a testimony. The spiritual witness that we call a *testimony* motivates us to act on Jesus's teachings and make the necessary changes in our lives to become true disciples of Jesus Christ, striving to become like Him in thought, word, and deed.

Elder David A. Bednar taught about the important interrelationship between testimony and conversion.

> Testimony is the *beginning of* and a *prerequisite* to continuing conversion. Testimony is a point of departure; it is not an ultimate destination. Strong testimony is the *foundation* upon which conversion is established.
>
> A testimony is [a] personal knowledge of spiritual truth obtained by revelation. . . . True conversion brings a change in one's beliefs, heart, and life to accept and conform to the will of God and includes a conscious commitment to become a disciple of Christ. . . . Conversion is an offering of self, of love, and of loyalty we give to God in gratitude for the gift of testimony. . . .
>
> . . . *Knowing that the gospel is true is the essence of a testimony. Consistently being true to the gospel is the essence of conversion.* We should know the gospel is true *and* be true to the gospel.[500]

Jesus asked a wealthy young ruler to give up all he had to follow Him, but this young man would not. We would suggest that he was not fully converted to Jesus. His testimony of the commandments led him to obey them; however, his partial conversion kept him from fully embracing faith in Jesus Christ and making the complete sacrifice the Savior asked him to make.[501]

At some point in our lives, each of us will have to answer the question of whether we are converted to Jesus and His gospel. We would suggest the answer does not lie in what we *know* or in what we *feel* but in what we *do* and who we *are*. Our choices, and ultimately our character, demonstrate our conversion.

Elder Jeffrey R. Holland once described a situation where a group of fans at a basketball game shouted epithets and criticism at a player who was a fellow member of the Church of Jesus Christ. When a reporter asked how they could do that, they said that when they came to a basketball game, they "checked their religion at the door." To this, Elder Holland vehemently responded, "You never 'check your religion at the door.' *Not ever!*"[502]

Individuals who are fully converted do not put their faith in Jesus aside—at school, at work, at the computer while privately in their room on the internet, or at any other time or in any other place. Full conversion does not require *fanaticism*, it requires *consistency*. Our hope is that we will consistently strive to live our testimony of Him, thus demonstrating our full conversion—our deep desire—to Jesus Christ and His gospel.

FINDING POWER IN HIM

Conversion to Jesus enables us to find power in our faith. That power will prompt us to do much good for others. It will enable us to wrestle with doubts and unknowns and move forward anyway. It will help us bless and serve others. It will give us peace and spiritual harmony. A mighty change of *heart* doesn't automatically mean a mighty change of *capability*. We may still have much to experience on our life's path to develop spiritually, but our faith in Jesus and our commitment to Him will give us power well beyond our natural abilities.

So many times, we have looked back on our lives and wondered how we got through the hard without breaking—whether it was illness, job loss, offensive or abusive comments and actions by others, or anything else that's happened to us. The only thing to which we can attribute the positive outcome is our faith in Jesus. Our natural capabilities never would have enabled us to accomplish what we achieved.

Aaron: As a freshman in 1989, I entered BYU only recently having been ordained an elder in the Melchizedek Priesthood. As with all newly ordained elders, my preparation to accept the oath and covenant of the higher priesthood came throughout my years as an Aaronic Priesthood holder. But I was not fully prepared to use it until I was asked. My first opportunity came during my first weeks at BYU.

We had come home from classes, and two friends from our stake came by to visit me and my roommate. We talked for a time, and my roommate decided to go for a short run. He left while the rest of us stayed behind chatting. After about twenty minutes, my roommate came back to the room in a bit of a panic. He said that he had been on his run, and, without explanation, he began to get hives all over his body.

His skin looked like it had hundreds of little bumps on it. Not knowing what to do, he asked us if we would give him a blessing. I looked at my other friends, who appeared to be just as panicked as I was. None of us had ever given a blessing before. I don't remember exactly how it happened, but one of our friends offered to perform the anointing, and I offered to do the blessing.

We got out our priesthood manual and quickly reviewed the procedure. My friend laid his hands on my roommate's head and anointed him with consecrated oil. Then, I laid my hands on his head to seal the anointing and give the blessing. I don't remember what I said. However, I do remember thinking about Jesus and hoping He would help me.

I can assure you that there was no more inadequate blessing given in the history of blessings. I am sure that my words lacked eloquence and finesse as I stuttered and stammered my way through the ordinance. However, I said what I felt, and I ended the blessing. Then, a miracle occurred. No sooner had I ended the blessing than my roommate's hives almost disappeared! Within a few minutes, his skin looked like he never had them in the first place.

We were all amazed by what had taken place. Here we were, young elders without much experience or knowledge, calling down the powers of heaven to bless one of our own with the simple faith that Jesus would help us. That blessing was honored by a loving Heavenly Father who, in His mercy, felt inclined to heal our friend.

I then realized that this authority that I held—this precious power—was not mine. It was from my Heavenly Father. He, not I, had healed my roommate. I knew for certain that I did little to have this miracle occur. My only task was to have faith in Jesus. Heavenly Father took care of the rest.

This experience has given me great comfort throughout my life. It has given me the peace of knowing that if I have complete faith in Jesus, I will have power to accomplish any task He asks of me.

BECOMING LIKE HIM

Our great task of this mortal probation is to learn to become like our Father in Heaven and His Son. The experiences we have during mortality are intended to provide us with the necessary clinical material to help us gain knowledge, turn that knowledge into experience, then ultimately use that experience to develop the traits and characteristics of Deity. Why? Because these traits are what will be necessary for us to accomplish God's eternal work of "bring[ing] to pass the immortality and eternal life of man,"[503] both in this life and in the next. Having the character of Christ is the very definition of harmony.

The Atonement of Jesus Christ is the great redeeming and enabling power required to accomplish this most important of all achievements: to become like our Father in Heaven. Through His sacrifice and resurrection, He offers all men and women immortality via resurrection. He can also protect or cover us from the effects of our sins and transgressions. This concept is the very meaning of the Hebrew word that is translated *atonement*. He has already paid the full price for our sins. Our duty in taking advantage of that redeeming power is to repent and to come to Him "with full purpose of heart."[504] In this way, He can truly become our Redeemer.

Jesus's Atonement also provides us with the strength to overcome our weaknesses, the power to develop attributes of kindness, love, patience, and humility, and the capability to serve others and to bear their burdens. Step by step, as we seek for and depend on the strengthening power of the Atonement, our meager efforts will be magnified, and we will be able to develop magnificent eternal traits. Ultimately, not only will we measure up, but we will come "unto the measure of the stature of the fulness of Christ."[505]

Julie: We have encountered many members of the Church who have LGBTQ family members. As they work through what this situation might mean for them, we are so impressed by those who find a way to allow their faith and Jesus Christ to guide their decisions. In the best cases, they find harmony in both loving their family members and holding fast to their faith in Jesus. Those who come to this harmony are changed even amid apparent incongruities.

Dr. Julia Campbell Bernards, who earned her doctorate from BYU, studied families with children who experience gender dysphoria to determine the effect of spirituality on them. Her unique research found a tie between the spirituality of these families and their ability to become more like their Heavenly Father despite the difficulty of their situation. She noted,

> The parents in our study primarily conceptualized their journey in spiritual terms. For them, their transformation wasn't consciously about achieving greater cognitive complexity, rewriting mental maps, or transcending socially constructed meanings; it was an opportunity to develop as a human being and make progress in their life's purpose—to better understand and become more like God.
>
> Even though parents' process was often messy and miserable, the meaning they made of it transformed it. They said,
>
> - "You will pass through [this process] and come out with a greater capacity to love and a greater understanding of God."
> - "[This process] is a good thing, it's a wonderful thing, it's, it's a miracle."
> - "On this journey [we] have experienced immeasurable personal and spiritual growth."

- "It has brought the Spirit into my life so much. . . . There is nothing that has blessed my life more."

> As parents aligned with personal spiritual experiences and made new meanings based on those experiences, shame and fear turned to hope and confidence. Even one of Latter-day Saint parents' most profound fears—losing their child spiritually—was allayed as they sought spiritual answers.
>
> As [one parent concluded], "This whole journey—it was sacred. I mean, it was . . . one of the most spiritual parts of my life."[506]

This sacred journey to arrive at harmony has been traversed by many who love their LGBTQ family and friends. These disciples demonstrate how to truly love God *and* love neighbor, which is the harmony that Jesus asked all disciples to achieve.

BE YE THEREFORE PERFECT, EVENTUALLY

As we mentioned earlier, a mighty change is made up of many mini changes. We are all in different places on our road to full conversion to Jesus. That's okay. We're okay. Imperfection is not failure. With intent to move forward, our current imperfection can be a positive indication that simply points us back to Jesus. To continue forward, we might want to start with the mini changes—those interim inflection points—that keep us on the road to a full conversion.

What choices are we making that demonstrate some aspect of conversion to the gospel of Jesus Christ? Do we choose to be kind, gentle, and loving to those around us? Do we choose to read scriptures and pray? Do we choose to serve another person and lift them up? Are we trying to be obedient to God? Above all, do we strive to make Jesus the center of what we do and who we are trying to become?

Christian traits—however imperfectly we demonstrate them—are a most important consideration. Elder Neal A. Maxwell noted,

> For the serious disciple, the cardinal attributes exemplified by Jesus are not optional. These developmental milestones take the form of traits, traits that mark the trail to be traveled. After all, should not Latter-day Saints have a

> special interest in what is required to become a Saint, virtue by virtue and quality by quality?"[507]

We must be patient with ourselves as we develop these traits. They will come slowly and over time as we follow Jesus. If we are frustrated with our progress, we shouldn't be! We should be as patient with ourselves as we are with others. And we must strive to be more patient with others—especially with those whom we love the most—when they falter on their road of discipleship. These words from Elder Jeffrey R. Holland can give us encouragement:

> Around the Church I hear many who struggle with this issue: "I am just not good enough." "I fall so far short." "I will never measure up." . . . Every one of us aspires to a more Christlike life than we often succeed in living. If we admit that honestly and are trying to improve, we are not hypocrites; we are human.
>
> May we refuse to let our own mortal follies, and the inevitable shortcomings of even the best men and women around us, make us cynical about the truths of the gospel, the truthfulness of the Church, our hope for our future, or the possibility of godliness. If we persevere, then somewhere in eternity our refinement will be finished and complete—which is the New Testament meaning of *perfection*.[508]

Julie: A good friend of ours who was diagnosed with multiple sclerosis shared with us a story of how his faith in Jesus helps him deal with a condition that has left him physically imperfect but spiritually perfecting. We share the story with his permission.

> I was taught from an early age to be grateful for Jesus Christ's atoning sacrifice. I was also taught to rely upon Him to help me through challenges or adversity. I will admit, however, that I didn't have a lot of hardships. While some things were daunting at the time, with hindsight I see that the challenges I faced in my younger years were almost trivial compared with trials that came later.
>
> Shortly after my forty-first birthday, I was diagnosed with multiple sclerosis (MS). There was no specific

prognosis; MS doesn't work that way. I did know that I had new physical limitations that would likely worsen over time. I sought blessings of healing. Loved ones prayed for me and I prayed for myself. I hoped that my faith in Christ would remove this disease.

Despite my faith and an aggressive treatment regimen, the MS worsened, and my walking, vision, and voice sharply deteriorated. I fought daily bouts of disabling fatigue. Within eighteen months, I had to stop working. It was very discouraging. What was I missing? What was I not doing right?

A friend shared a helpful insight. She had dealt with similar challenges and questions. She suggested that being *healed* was not necessarily synonymous with being *cured*. Wait. What? Could I be *healed* even if the MS continued unabated? Yes.

In fact, I believe I have been healed through a combination of faith in Christ and the healing power of His priesthood. The turbulence caused by the unknown has been calmed, even though the future is still undetermined. The anxiety that resulted from my new limitations has been quelled, even though the physical weakness remains. As so many doors of opportunity were quickly closing, I used to be enveloped in gloom. But that sadness has completely dissipated, even though those doors remain closed. And even better, I've found new opportunities and new strengths.

During the early months of my disease, I felt that MS was an interruption to my life. As part of the healing process, I recognized that this health challenge was not an interruption *to* my life; it was a foundational part *of* my life. I began to understand that my response to this adversity would help define me, refine me, and if I endured it well, would serve as a priceless blessing to me and my family.

To be clear, the healing and peace did not happen overnight. The physical challenges did not slacken. In fact, they intensified. What was healed was my perspective, my attitude, and my outlook, whatever course the MS took.

> The gratitude I feel for the Savior and my reliance on Him to succor me have coalesced in beautiful harmony.[509]

Our friend has found harmony in his life despite his continued challenges. Likewise, our mighty change—and many mini changes like he saw—can provide us a place of peace amid life's challenges. Harmony isn't the end of our journey of faith. It's a new beginning.

Navigating to Jesus is a lifelong journey of faith. Finding harmony in Him will happen repeatedly—with minor *harmonies* early in our journey giving way to major *symphonies* later. This repetitive process is what brings us an amplification of joy. It's what allows us to become more like our heavenly parents. It's what will eventually bring us to our heavenly home.

QUESTIONS TO CONSIDER

1. What are the mini changes that could bring you harmony as you progress on your journey of faith?
2. How are you showing your conversion to the Lord? What changes—large or small—are you trying to make to increase your faith in Jesus?
3. What is something that you are seeking power to overcome? How can your faith in Jesus enable you to accomplish it?
4. What would a mighty change look like in your life? How can you continue towards it?
5. How can you find greater patience with your journey of faith? How can you be comfortable with where you are and still have the desire to make further changes?

NOTES AND INSIGHTS

EPILOGUE
COME UNTO CHRIST

Come unto me, all ye that labour and are heavy laden,
and I will give you rest. Take my yoke upon you,
and learn of me . . . and ye shall find
rest unto your souls.

—MATTHEW 11:28–29

We conclude this book with a simple invitation to all who read it: "Come unto Christ and be perfected in Him."[510] As you navigate to Jesus and traverse your journey of faith, we know that He will walk with you. He will guide you in your confusion. He will comfort you in your distress. He will answer you in your doubts. We leave you with three promises:

- His grace is sufficient
- His love is abounding
- His redemption is sure

HIS GRACE IS SUFFICIENT

First, we promise you that Jesus's grace is sufficient.[511] He can resolve every injury, illness, sin, unfairness, abuse, or difficulty you or anyone you know could ever experience. He has all power to save. As your faith in Him grows, you will see greater and greater expressions of that grace—of His tender mercies.

At times, we have felt like the Lord has forgotten us. When we have felt hopeless, lost, and disregarded in our lives, we have come to recognized that we have lost sight of His infinite and abundant grace. When we renew our faith in Him and trust in that grace, our fears subside, and our ability to progress returns.

Aaron. Several years ago, my mother went back to her home city in the Philippines to visit her relatives. One evening while she was at her ancestral home, she received a visit from her mother's first cousin, Veronica Juni.

Veronica was then ninety-five years old. She stood not quite five feet tall. Her eyes had dimmed due to cataracts, and she hunched when she stood due to her advanced age. She used a small bamboo pole as a cane to help steady her when she walked.

Veronica lived alone. All her children were grown and lived away from her. She still cooked her own meals and cleaned her own house. Sometimes she sat out near the big mango tree in the front of her home and listened to the children who played in her yard. They called her Lula, which means "grandmother" in my mother's native dialect.

When Veronica heard from the grandchildren that my mother had come to visit, she decided to come and see my mom. Veronica's house was about a quarter of a mile away from where my mother was staying, and she walked the entire distance along a busy highway, slowly making her way using her bamboo cane.

My mom and Veronica had a wonderful visit. As they conversed, my mother was amazed at how long Veronica had lived and that she still did so many things on her own. "Lula," my mother asked, "how is it that you have lived so long?" With a sigh and a shake of her head, Veronica replied, "I don't know. I guess God just forgot about me."

This response touched my mother deeply. At the end of their visit, she watched as this sweet lady made her way down the highway, slowly walking with her bamboo cane back to her little house, to live out the rest of her days alone, thinking that somehow God had forgotten about her.

We want to say to Veronica, and to all of you, that God has not forgotten you! He loves you as His precious child with eternal potential. Know that His grace is sufficient for you.

To us, Jesus says, "Fear thou not; for *I am with thee*: be not dismayed; for I am thy God: I will *strengthen* thee; yea, I will *help* thee; yea, I will *uphold* thee with the right hand of my righteousness."[512]

HIS LOVE IS ABOUNDING

Second, we promise you that Jesus's love is abounding. Jesus does not exclude anyone from His love. "He inviteth them all to come unto him and partake of his goodness; and he denieth none that come unto him, black and white, bond and free, male and female; and he remembereth the [unbeliever]; and all are alike unto God."[513] Love is connection, and Jesus desires to connect with everyone. All can feel a sense of belonging with Him.

If you feel like you are an outsider for any reason, know that Jesus's love is abounding. He often manifests His love through others. When you think of the many who know and love you, the cumulative expressions of their love can give you a small sense of the infinite love Jesus has for you. Hold on to any small portion of that love until He can find ways to send you more.

To us Jesus says, "I have loved thee with an *everlasting love*: therefore with lovingkindness have I drawn thee [to me]."[514]

HIS REDEMPTION IS SURE

Third, we promise you that Jesus's redemption is sure. Elder Patrick Kearon taught, "God is in relentless pursuit of you. He 'wants all of His children to choose to return to Him,' and He employs every possible measure to bring you back."[515] He won't stop until the blessing, comfort, and resolution you need are in your grasp. He won't quit until you are in His arms. His redemption efforts are sure!

You may think, "My problems are impossible to solve," or "I'm too far gone to help." Peter, the Lord's chief Apostle, could have had these thoughts. At a most critical moment, he denied the Christ. After his third denial, Jesus turned to look at him. Realizing what he had done, Peter went out and wept bitterly.[516] He still loved the Lord, but in a moment of weakness, he denied his faith out of fear. The look from His Lord was a look of love, not condemnation. The Lord loved him anyway and waited for him to "come unto himself."[517] Peter needed this painful event to become the rock that the Lord needed to lead His fledgling Church.

If you don't think the issues in your life can be resolved, remember that Jesus's redemption is sure. He will find a way to bring peace back to your life. He will wait on you and will not condemn you in your weakness. He will heal your pain. His redemption may come in an unexpected manner, but we assure you that it *will* come. And you will be stronger for it. To us Jesus says,

> Fear not: for *I have redeemed thee*, I have called thee by thy name; *thou art mine*. When thou passest through the waters, *I will be with thee*; and through the rivers, they shall not overflow thee: when thou walkest through the fire, thou shalt not be burned; neither shall the flame kindle upon thee. For *I* am the Lord *thy* God, the Holy One of Israel, *thy* Saviour.[518]

BEAUTY FOR ASHES

This book has been a labor of love for us. We feel compelled to testify of Jesus because His love, mercy, and grace have been so abundant through the course of our journey of faith. We have remained true to Him despite our doubts and heartaches, and in return, He has blessed us beyond our expectations.

As we wrote, the words came *to* us more than they came *from* us. We were honored to be ministers of Jesus in this small way as He guided us. Through Isaiah, the Redeemer proclaimed His saving work:

> The Spirit of the Lord God is upon me; because the Lord hath anointed me to preach good tidings unto the meek; he hath sent me to bind up the *brokenhearted*, to proclaim liberty to the *captives*, and the opening of the prison to them that are *bound*;
>
> To proclaim the acceptable year of the Lord, and the day of vengeance of our God; *to comfort all that mourn*;

> To appoint unto them that mourn in Zion, to give unto them *beauty for ashes, the oil of joy for mourning, the garment of praise for the spirit of heaviness*; that they might be called trees of righteousness, the planting of the Lord, that he might be glorified.
>
> And they shall build the old wastes, they shall raise up the former desolations, and they shall repair the waste cities, the desolations of many generations.[519]

As witnesses of Jesus, our Redeemer, we share His Light by joining with Him in proclaiming good tidings to all and binding up the broken hearted. We wrote this book to help you build or rebuild the waste places in your life through your faith in Jesus. We've had to do it in our lives, so we know the work this takes. We also understand the beauty that can come from these efforts.

We have on our mantel a very special item. It is a beautiful glass egg with swirls of colors in it. Anyone who has seen it has marveled at its beauty. This piece was made from the ashes of Mount St. Helens which violently erupted on May 18, 1980.

The volcanic eruption that happened over forty years ago was horrific. Ash from the volcano was deposited in eleven US states. Almost sixty people were killed, and hundreds of square miles were reduced to wasteland. The devastation was immense as was the tragedy.

Yet out of the ashes from this terrible event came this beautiful piece of art. By putting these ashes under extreme pressure, the artist created a thing of beauty. Jesus can do the same for us. The pressure of our trials may feel immense, but the character that will emerge when we focus on Jesus Christ will be a thing of beauty. Truly Jesus will give to us "beauty for ashes" and the "oil of joy for mourning."[520]

We testify that Jesus lives. He lives! He loves us. He is our Savior and Redeemer who offers us salvation through His grace. We believe in His life and ministry. We have faith in His doctrine. We know Him in our extremities. Our personal experience with Jesus has been born in our personal suffering, in our deepest pleadings and struggles, and in our complete submission to His will. We have seen the ashes in our lives break forth into beauty in miraculous ways because of Him.

We invite you to come unto Jesus Christ. Seek Him. Follow Him. And we promise He will come unto you and bring you the harmony and peace you seek as He has for us.

May you find joy on your journey of faith as you navigate to Jesus!

APPENDIX A
JOURNEYS OF FAITH

We found God's pattern of faith recorded repeatedly in our canonized scriptures. We chose three examples to share here, but the scriptures contain many more. We chose to share how Enos, Alma the Younger, and Paul described their most significant conversion experiences. Our summary is shown in the table that follows.

God's Pattern	Enos	Alma	Paul
Experience an Opposition	"I will tell you of the wrestle which I had before God, before I received a remission of my sins."[521]	"I fell to the earth; and it was for the space of three days and three nights that I could not open my mouth, neither had I the use of my limbs."[522]	"Suddenly there shone from heaven a great alight round about me. And I fell unto the ground."[523]
Awaken Unto God	"My soul hungered."[524]	"I was racked with eternal torment, for my soul was harrowed up to the greatest degree and racked with all my sins. … [For] I saw that I had rebelled against my God, and that I had not kept his holy commandments."[525]	"[I was] trembling and astonished"[526] and "When I was come again to Jerusalem, even while I prayed in the temple, I was in a trance."[527]

God's Pattern	Enos	Alma	Paul
Know God's Plan of Mercy	"The words which I had often heard my father speak concerning eternal life, and the joy of the saints, sunk deep into my heart."[528]	"I remembered also to have heard my father prophesy unto the people concerning the coming of one Jesus Christ, a Son of God, to atone for the sins of the world."[529]	"Rise, and stand upon thy feet: for I have appeared unto thee for this purpose, to make thee a minister and a witness both of these things which thou hast seen."[530]
Seek This Jesus	"I cried unto [the Lord] in mighty prayer and supplication for mine own soul."[531]	"I cried within my heart: O Jesus, thou Son of God, have mercy on me, who am in the gall of bitterness, and am encircled about by the everlasting chains of death."[532]	"Who art thou, Lord? And he said unto me, I am Jesus of Nazareth, whom thou persecutest. … And I said, What shall I do, Lord?"[533]
Believe on Him	"I, Enos, knew that God could not lie."[534]	"I do put my trust in him, and he will still deliver me."[535]	"[Paul] spake boldly in the name of Jesus."[536]
Act on Faith In Him	"All the day long did I cry unto him … Because of [my] faith in Christ."[537]	"I do know, that inasmuch as ye shall keep the commandments of God ye shall prosper in the land."[538]	"And I said, What shall I do, Lord? … I was not disobedient unto the heavenly vision."[539]
Always Remember Him	"I cried unto him continually, for he had said unto me: Whatsoever thing ye shall ask in faith, believing that ye shall receive in the name of Christ, ye shall receive it."[540]	"I will praise him forever, for he has brought our fathers out of Egypt … and he has delivered them out of bondage and captivity … and I have always retained [this] in remembrance."[541]	"I [witness] both to small and great … That Christ should suffer, and that he should be the first that should brise from the dead, and should shew light unto the people, and to the Gentiles."[542]

God's Pattern	Enos	Alma	Paul
Endure in Faith on His Name	"I have declared it in all my days."[543]	"I have been supported under trials and troubles of every kind, yea, and in all manner of afflictions; yea, God has delivered me from prison, and from bonds, and from death."[544]	"I continue unto this day, witnessing both to small and great, saying none other things than those which the prophets and Moses did say should come."[545]
Minister in His Love	"I began to feel a desire for the welfare of my brethren."[546]	"I have labored without ceasing, that I might bring souls unto repentance; that I might bring them to taste of the exceeding joy of which I did taste."[547]	"[I] shewed first unto them of Damascus, and at Jerusalem, and throughout all the coasts of Judæa, and then to the Gentiles, that they should repent and turn to God, and do works meet for repentance."[548]
Witness a Mighty Change	"My faith began to be unshaken in the Lord. … And I rejoice in the day when my mortal shall put on immor-tality, and shall stand before him; then shall I see his face with pleasure."[549]	"I could remember my pains no more; yea, I was harrowed up by the memory of my sins no more. And oh, what joy, and what marvelous light I did behold; yea, my soul was filled with joy as exceeding as was my pain!"[550]	"I have fought a good fight, I have finished my course, I have kept the faith."[551]

APPENDIX B
YOUR JOURNEY TO FAITH

You can write your own journey of spiritual growth by filling out the table on the following pages for yourself. Answer each question for a particular event that has occurred or is currently occurring in your life. This exercise will help keep you focused on the Savior and will allow you to monitor and record your progress.

God's Pattern	Key Question for You
Experience an Opposition	What opposition (difficulty or ease) did you face?
Your Growth Event	
Awaken Unto God	What did you come to realize about yourself and your Savior?
Your Growth Event	
Know God's Plan of Mercy	How did your situation fit into God's plan of mercy for you?
Your Growth Event	
Seek This Jesus	How did you seek the Savior in your opposition?
Your Growth Event	
Believe on Him	In what way did you simply believe in Jesus?
Your Growth Event	

God's Pattern	Key Question for You
Act on Faith in Him	How did you act on faith in Him, without a complete knowledge?
Your Growth Event	
Always Remember Him	In what ways did you remember Jesus and His mercy?
Your Growth Event	
Endure in Faith on His Name	How did you endure in faith on the Savior?
Your Growth Event	
Minister in His Love	How did you minister to others in similitude of the Savior?
Your Growth Event	
Witness a Mighty Change	What mighty change occurred in your heart?
Your Growth Event	

ENDNOTES

1. For example, positive attitudes, family support, social networks, professional counseling, personal resilience, etc.
2. Nelson, "Joy and Spiritual Survival."
3. William Blake, Soren Keirkegaard, William Perry, and James Fowler are among the many writers who have proposed stages of faith. For example, James Fowler proposes six stages of faith in his book *Stages of Faith: The Psychology of Human Development and the Quest for Meaning.* Readers would benefit from studying others' approaches.
4. McLaren, *Faith After Doubt,* 2021. See Appendix I for a summary of his four stages of faith. McLaren maps his stages to those offered by other authors in Appendix III of his book.
5. McLaren, "Your Faith Isn't Broken."
6. McLaren, *Faith,* 104–115.
7. See McLaren, 41–48.
8. See McLaren, 48–63.
9. See McLaren, 63–93.
10. See Alma 24:30.
11. See McLaren, 93–102.
12. "Faith is things which are hoped for and not seen; wherefore, dispute not because ye see not, for ye receive no witness until after the trial of your faith" (Ether 12:6).
13. See 1 Nephi 10:17; Joseph Smith—History 1:20.
14. See Mosiah 5:2.
15. John 3:3. See also Mosiah 27:25–26.
16. Doctrine and Covenants 76:53.
17. Bednar, "A Reservoir of Living Water."
18. See Mosiah 3 for the full account.
19. See Mosiah 4:1–3.
20. Mosiah 5:2.
21. In appendix A, we also provide a summary of three case studies from the scriptures where this pattern is observed: Enos, Alma the Younger, and Paul.
22. Mosiah 4:2. See also 2 Nephi 2:11.
23. Mosiah 4:5.
24. Mosiah 4:6.
25. Mosiah 4:8.
26. Mosiah 4:9.

27. Mosiah 4:10, 12.
28. Mosiah 4:11.
29. Mosiah 4:12.
30. Mosiah 4:15–16.
31. Mosiah 5:2–3.
32. Colossians 1:17, Revised Standard Version.
33. See Matthew 3:17; 3 Nephi 11, 17; Joseph Smith—History 1:17.
34. Revelation 1:8; Doctrine and Covenants 19:1.
35. Hebrews 12:2; Moroni 6:4.
36. Doctrine and Covenants 88:6, 13.
37. 2 Nephi 11:4.
38. John 14:6.
39. See 2 Nephi 31:21; Mosiah 3:17; Alma 38:9; Helaman 5:9.
40. Nelson, "The Answer Is Always Jesus Christ."
41. Moses 7:21.
42. See Helaman 5:12.
43. McLaren, *Faith.* Picture of Jesus Christ is *Christ at 33*, Heinrich Hoffman (1824–1911). © Riverside Church, New York, NY.
44. Mosiah 3:17.
45. 2 Corinthians 12:9; Ether 12:26; Doctrine and Covenants 18:31.
46. 2 Nephi 2:11.
47. Isaiah 9:2.
48. Alma 31:5; emphasis added.
49. Matthew 25:14–30.
50. Matthew 25:23.
51. Matthew 25:26.
52. Gravitropism is also known as geotropism.
53. Tiwari, "Seed."
54. Ibid.
55. 2 Nephi 2:11.
56. Jacob 4:13.
57. Maxwell, "If Thou Endure It Well."
58. See 2 Nephi 2:12.
59. See Jacob 6:12.
60. 2 Nephi 2:15–16.
61. Isaiah 3:15; 2 Nephi 13:15.
62. Kimball, *Tragedy or Destiny?*, 2–3.
63. Maxwell, "If Thou Endure It Well."
64. 2 Nephi 2:13.
65. Helaman 3:29–30.
66. 2 Nephi 2:12.
67. "Wisdom," *Oxford Dictionary of English,* 2036.
68. Mosiah 4:27.
69. Alma 42:22; Mormon 9:19.

70. 2 Nephi 2:12.
71. Boyd K. Packer, Kingsland Georgia Stake Conference, August 1997 as quoted by Lynn G. Robbins in "Until Seventy Times Seven." Report, April 2018.
72. Romans 8:28; see also Doctrine and Covenants 90:24.
73. Hebrews 12:11; emphasis added.
74. See Doctrine and Covenants 122:7.
75. We wrote our first book, *Discovering Your Temple Insights,* while trapped in our house during the COVID-19 pandemic.
76. "Power," *Oxford Dictionary of English,* 1393.
77. Moses 1:39.
78. Joseph Smith taught, "By this we understand that the principle of power which existed in the bosom of God, by which the worlds were framed, was faith; and that it is by reason of this principle of power existing in the Deity, that all created things exist; so that all things in heaven, on earth, or under the earth, exist by reason of faith as it existed in HIM. . . . It is the principle by which Jehovah works, and through which he exercises power over all temporal as well as eternal things" (Joseph Smith, *Lectures on Faith,* 1:15–16, 8–9).
79. See Doctrine and Covenants 29:36. In this verse, we learn that the adversary tried to usurp that power in the premortal war. Lucifer did not understand that honor—or trust—is developed, not taken.
80. See Doctrine and Covenants 88:109.
81. See Doctrine and Covenants 121:41–43. *Unfeigned* means authentic or genuine.
82. Doctrine and Covenants 76:24.
83. Bruce R. McConkie, "The Purifying Power of Gethsemane."
84. See 2 Nephi 32:8.
85. Doctrine and Covenants 84:20.
86. Alma 62:41.
87. See Luke 15:10–32 for the story of the prodigal son and his loving father.
88. Matthew 7:7; Luke 11:9; 3 Nephi 14:7.
89. Doctrine and Covenants 64:10; emphasis added.
90. 2 Nephi 19:9.
91. J. Reuben Clark, Conference Report, October 1953, 84.
92. Revelation 15:3.
93. Alma 7:12.
94. Ezra Taft Benson, "Beware of Pride."
95. Alma 5:7.
96. See John 1:1; Mosiah 24:14.
97. Mosiah 5:2.
98. 2 Nephi 31:13; see also Mosiah 7:33; 3 Nephi 10:6; 18:32.
99. See Alma 32:13–16.
100. Isaiah 55:8–9.
101. Moroni 10:32.
102. See Matthew 5:25.
103. See Matthew 5:39.

104. See Matthew 5:44.
105. See Matthew 7:1.
106. See Matthew 7:3.
107. See Matthew 7:12.
108. Alma 5:7.
109. John 1:1–5; see also Doctrine and Covenants 6:21; 93:8–9.
110. 1 John 1:5.
111. John 8:12.
112. Alma 26:15; Doctrine and Covenants 95:12.
113. See John 3:16.
114. 2 Nephi 1:15; emphasis added. See also Alma 36:20.
115. Ecclesiastes 11:7.
116. Mosiah 5:3.
117. John 14:26.
118. John 1:1–5; see also Doctrine and Covenants 6:21; 93:8–9.
119. Doctrine and Covenants 84:45; emphasis added.
120. Doctrine and Covenants 93:24.
121. See Jacob 4:13. "Things" can be changed to "people."
122. Doctrine and Covenants 50:24, changing the word "love" for "light."
123. Mosiah 4:5.
124. Abraham 3:24–25; emphasis added.
125. Mosiah 15:3.
126. 2 Corinthians 12:7.
127. For example, some of us may be clumsy, tend to procrastinate, or be easily distracted. Some weaknesses can be more disruptive to our lives such as when issues associated with our physical or mental health prevent us from fully functioning at work or at home.
128. See Dallin H. Oaks, "Sins and Mistakes," BYU Speeches, August 16, 1994, for a detailed treatment of the difference between sins and mistakes.
129. "What Is Alcohol Use Disorder?"; emphasis added.
130. Ether 12:27; emphasis added.
131. Nelson, "Choices for Eternity."
132. See 2 Nephi 26:23; Doctrine and Covenants 93:36.
133. Alma 32:35.
134. Romans 13:12.
135. "Spiritual Gifts," Topics and Questions.
136. Doctrine and Covenants 46:11.
137. Moses 1:39.
138. Isaiah 49:2.
139. Doctrine and Covenants 59:21.
140. See Moroni 7:39–47.
141. Gary B. Sabin, "Hallmarks of Happiness."
142. Richard G. Scott, "Finding the Joy in Life."
143. Taylor, *Life Is Incredibly Unfair, in Our Favor.*

144. See Alma 12:30; 24:14; Moses 6:62.
145. The nine names for God's plan in the Book of Mormon are (1) merciful plan of the great Creator (2 Nephi 9:6), (2) plan of our God (2 Nephi 9:13), (3) plan of deliverance (2 Nephi 11:5), (4) plan of redemption (Jacob 6:8; Alma 12:25–26, 30, 32–33; 17:16; 18:39; 22:13; 34:16, 31; 39:18; 42:11, 13), (5) plan of salvation (Jarom 1:2; Alma 24:14; 29:2; 42:5), (6) great plan (Alma 34:9), (7) plan of restoration (Alma 41:2), (8) plan of happiness (Alma 42:8, 16), and (9) plan of mercy (Alma 42:15, 31).
146. Alma 42:14.
147. Moses 1:39.
148. For a more complete treatment of God's plan of salvation, see "Chapter 3, Lesson 2: Heavenly Father's Plan of Salvation," *Preach My Gospel: A Guide to Sharing the Gospel of Jesus Christ,* 2023.
149. 3 Nephi 19:27; see also Moses 6:57.
150. Alma 7:11–12.
151. Jesus only made three statements in The New Testament where He used the word *saved.* (1) Enter by the door (Jesus) and be saved (see John 10:9), (2) He that believeth and is baptized shall be saved (see Mark 16:16); later He clarified that we needed to be born of water and the Spirit (see John 3:3–5), and (3) He that endures to the end will be saved (see Matthew 10:22, 24:13; Mark 13:13). These actions to be saved by Jesus are the doctrine of Christ."
152. Revelation 12:11.
153. 2 Nephi 2:27.
154. See Moses 4:1–4.
155. "The Family: A Proclamation to the World."
156. 1 Nephi 11:17.
157. 2 Nephi 26:24.
158. 1 John 4:19.
159. See Helaman 14:30–31.
160. See 2 Nephi 2:16; emphasis added.
161. See 2 Nephi 2:27.
162. See Joseph Smith—History 1.
163. Matthew 28:19.
164. For a more complete treatment of the restoration of the gospel of Jesus Christ, see "Chapter 3, Lesson 1: The Message of the Restoration of the Gospel of Jesus Christ," *Preach My Gospel: A Guide to Sharing the Gospel of Jesus Christ,* 2023.
165. The Book of Mormon documents two such scatterings: the people of the brother of Jared and the Nephites. Additionally in Jacob 5, we are given an extended allegory of the wild and the tame olive trees, which tells the story of scattering and gathering and how this process ensures that the root (the covenant) does not die.
166. Nelson, "Hope of Israel."
167. The Father always declares, "This is my beloved Son in whom I am well pleased," adding, "Hear Him!" following His resurrection (see Matthew 3: 17; Mark 1:113; Nephi 11:7; Joseph Smith—History 1:18).

168. We looked up every talk given by President Russell M. Nelson since he was called as our prophet and found that the overriding theme of his discourses was Jesus Christ. We grouped like discourses together, and put them in the following four categories: (1) become like Him, (2) covenant with Him, (3) hear Him, and (4) gather all to Him. We believe that President Nelson has given us a newly inspired way to frame the plan of salvation.
169. Joseph Smith—History 1:17.
170. See Doctrine and Covenants 1:39.
171. Doctrine and Covenants 1:38; emphasis added.
172. We should not provide counsel for anyone outside of our areas of stewardship. Revelation from God can only come to us for our own areas of stewardship. If we receive information for areas outside our stewardship, we can know with assurance that this prompting is not from God.
173. The Lord states that "the weak things of the world shall come forth" and be called. He then gives us six reasons He calls weak, fallible men and women in His work: (1) that people will not counsel each other and not trust in man, but seek counsel from and trust in God, (2) that every person might speak in the name of the Lord, (3) that faith might increase, (4) that His everlasting covenant might be established, (5) that the fulness of the gospel might be proclaimed to all, and (6) that weak servants may come to an understanding. If we understand these six points, we will be more understanding when we experience issues with leaders. The Lord then gives these weak servants four points they should understand: (1) know your errors (innocent mistakes, foibles) so you can correct them and the errors of others so you can forgive them, (2) receive instruction so you can increase in wisdom, (3) know your sins, so you can repent, and (4) be humble, so you can receive inspired knowledge and power from the Lord. If they follow these points, they will be more effective in their service.
174. Doctrine and Covenants 9:9.
175. Doctrine and Covenants 90:5.
176. See Doctrine and Covenants 8:2.
177. *History of the Church* 3:381.
178. Galatians 5:22–23.
179. Boyd K. Packer, "Prayer and Promptings."
180. Doctrine and Covenants 50:24.
181. Doctrine and Covenants 4:5.
182. Names in this story have been changed.
183. Hales, "Mortality Works."
184. Connie Goltz, email to authors, December 8, 2024.
185. I am surprised that opponents have repeated the same information for so long when much of it has been addressed, clarified, or refuted by apologetic research. I'm also amazed when members encounter information they think is new but has been used for a long time by opponents of the Church. For those seeking apologetic and scholarly responses to this kind of information, visit https://www.fairlatterdaysaints.org/.
186. Some of our dearest friends and family are members of other Christian denominations. We love their faith in Jesus and celebrate their Christian lives of goodness and

love. We are saddened and disappointed when others criticize our faith in Jesus as members of The Church of Jesus Christ of Latter-day Saints. We hope that all who have faith in Jesus Christ can love and support one another on their journeys of faith in Him.

187. See 2 Nephi 11:4; Jacob 4:5; Alma 33:19; Moses 6:63.
188. Jeremiah 29:13; emphasis added.
189. 1 Nephi 8:32. In Lehi's vision of the tree of life, the iron rod is the "word of God' (1 Nephi 11:25). Jesus is called the "Word" by the ancient apostle John (see John 1:1). Therefore, we might suggest that the iron rod is a representation of Jesus, just as it is a symbol of the scriptures, which are the words given through Jesus.
190. 2 Nephi 25: 28; emphasis added.
191. *Teaching in the Savior's Way,* Part 1: Focus on Jesus Christ.
192. See Doctrine and Covenants 90:24; Romans 8:28.
193. Helaman 5:12.
194. Jacob 4:14
195. Maxwell, "Jesus of Nazareth, Savior and King."
196. See Jacob 4:15.
197. Hebrews 12:2; see also Moroni 6:4.
198. Doctrine and Covenants 45:3.
199. Jacob 14:16.
200. John 14:18.
201. John 1:43; emphasis added. See also Matthew 9:9; Mark 2:14; Luke 5:27 for the invitation to Matthew.
202. Matthew 4:19; emphasis added.
203. Matthew 8:22; emphasis added. See also Luke 9:23.
204. John 10:25–27; emphasis added.
205. Matthew 16:24; emphasis added.
206. Matthew 19:21; emphasis added. See also Mark 10:21; Luke 18:22.
207. John 12:26; emphasis added.
208. John 21:15–18.
209. John 21:22; emphasis added.
210. 3 Nephi 12:48.
211. Matthew 11:28; emphasis added. See also 2 Nephi 26:25.
212. Matthew 19:14; emphasis added.
213. John 6:35; emphasis added.
214. John 7:37; emphasis added.
215. Matthew 11:29–30; emphasis added.
216. *Dialectical* refers to the interaction, tension, or resolution of opposing ideas, forces or concepts.
217. See Luke 18:15–17.
218. See Matthew 9:10–13.
219. See John 8:3–11.
220. See Matthew 23:13–33.
221. See Luke 20:22–25.

222. See Luke 20:1–8.
223. See Luke 17:11–14.
224. Matthew 23:4; Mark 7:1–7.
225. See John 2:1–11.
226. See John 19:25–27.
227. See Matthew 10:1–8.
228. See Matthew 25:69–75; 26:36–46; Mark 10:35–45; Luke 9:46–48; 51–56; John 20:24–29.
229. See Matthew 3:13–17.
230. See John 15:13–15.
231. See Matthew 16:21–23; Luke 9:51–56.
232. See John 6:59–69.
233. See Luke 12:51–53.
234. See John 17:21–22.
235. See Luke 22:41–44.
236. See Luke 2:52.
237. See Matthew 4:1–11.
238. See John 4:5–30.
239. See Matthew 20:28; John 3:16; 10:14–15.
240. See Matthew 4:1–2.
241. See Matthew 25:35–40.
242. See Luke 21:1–4.
243. See Matthew 26:6–13.
244. See Luke 17:11–19.
245. See Matthew 27:55–56; Luke 8:1–3; 23:49, 55–56; John 20:1–18.
246. See Matthew 21:12–13; John 2:13–16.
247. See Matthew 5:9, 23–24, 38–39, 44.
248. Jeffrey R. Holland, "I Am He." Report, October 2024.
249. Mark 6:22; emphasis added.
250. Mark 6:22.
251. See Luke 18:1–7.
252. Luke 18:5.
253. John 14:11; emphasis added.
254. See Matthew 28:18–20.
255. Mark 9:37; emphasis added.
256. 2 Corinthians 12:9; Ether 12:26; Doctrine and Covenants 18:31.
257. Revelation 3:20; emphasis added.
258. John 15:4; emphasis added.
259. "Abide," *Oxford Dictionary of English*, 3.
260. Holland, "Abide in Me."
261. John 6:60, 66.
262. John 6:67.
263. John 6:68–69.
264. See Luke 15:3–7.

265. Luke 15:6.
266. John 14:18; emphasis added.
267. Matthew 9:22.
268. John 14:23; emphasis added.
269. John 14:27; emphasis added.
270. John 16:7, 13; emphasis added.
271. Alma 32:27; emphasis added.
272. See Mosiah 4:9.
273. John 14:1.
274. Matthew 9:28; emphasis added.
275. Mark 5:36; emphasis added.
276. Mark 9:24; emphasis added.
277. John 4:48; emphasis added.
278. See John 11:1–46.
279. John 11:15; emphasis added.
280. The earlier raising of Jairus's daughter was kept secret. It was only known by Jesus, Jairus's family, and Peter, James, and John.
281. John 11:25–26; emphasis added.
282. John 11:27.
283. John 11:40; emphasis added.
284. John 11:45; emphasis added.
285. See Mark 5:25–34; Luke 8:43–48.
286. Mark 5:36; emphasis added; see also Luke 8:50.
287. See Mark 5:39.
288. See Mark 5:40–43.
289. Matthew 28:5.
290. 2 Corinthians 12:9; Ether 12:26; Doctrine and Covenants 18:31.
291. Doctrine and Covenants 6:36.
292. John 20:31; emphasis added.
293. 1 John 3:23; emphasis added.
294. See Moroni 4:3; Doctrine and Covenants 20:77.
295. See Doctrine and Covenants 107:23.
296. Bednar, "Special Witnesses of the Name of Christ."
297. See Acts 4:7.
298. John 8:12.
299. John 12:36; emphasis added.
300. Doctrine and Covenants 84:45; see also Doctrine and Covenants 93:36.
301 2 Nephi 28:14; see also Matthew 15:9; Doctrine and Covenants 93:39.
302. Doctrine and Covenants 11:11.
303. See Moroni 7:5–19.
304. See 2 Nephi 26:10.
305. John 8:12.
306. 1 John 1:5; emphasis added.
307. 1 John 1:7–8; emphasis added.

308. John 10:24–25; emphasis added.
309. John 10:37–38.
310. Matthew 7:20.
311. See Moroni 7:5–19.
312. We are not saying to ignore persistent or purposely abusive, threatening, or antagonistic behavior. None of these evil acts are acceptable. We are speaking of people who are striving to do good but who have imperfections.
313. John 14:12.
314. Evans, "Seeing Is Believing." Temple Insights Blog, July 31, 2024.
315. See Matthew 11:28–30; John 14:27; 16:33.
316. See John 14:16–17; 16:13; Acts 1:8.
317. See Matthew 7:7–8; Mark 11:24; John 14:13–14.
318. See Matthew 28:20; Luke 12:11–12; John 15:5.
319. See Matthew 6:14; Mark 2:10; John 8:36.
320. See Luke 10:19; John 8:12; 12:46.
321. See Matthew 11:28; John 14:1–2; Revelation 3:10.
322. See Matthew 25:21; John 15:11; 16:22.
323. See John 3:16; 6:40; 10:27–28.
324. Doctrine and Covenants 5:16.
325. John 12:47; emphasis added.
326. Isaiah 40:31.
327. 2 Nephi 33:10.
328. Kris Katseanes, "First Principles of the Gospel and Temple Covenants," Temple Insights Blog, December 7, 2022.
329. Matthew 21:22; Mark 11:24, emphasis added.
330. Christofferson, "Our Relationship with God."
331. Wilcox, "Book of Mormon, Episode 40: 3 Nephi 12–16, Part 2," timestamp 20:55; emphasis added.
332. See Matthew 6:9–13.
333. See Mark 9:14–29.
334. Mark 9:22; emphasis added.
335. Mark 9:23; emphasis added.
336. Mark 9:24; emphasis added.
337. John 10:27; emphasis added.
338. The family prefers to remain anonymous.
339. Bible Dictionary, "Faith"; emphasis added.
340. James 2:17–18; emphasis added.
341. Monson, "The Master's Blueprint."
342. Alma 32:21.
343. Joseph B. Wirthlin, "Shall He Find Faith on the Earth?"; emphasis added.
344. Hebrews 11:1; emphasis added. *Substance* means assurance.
345. Alma 32:15–16.
346. See Moroni 7:48.
347. Articles of Faith 1:4.

348. We use the term *darkness* to represent unknowns, confusion, doubt, distress, or any other situation or condition where we are unsure, uncertain, or confused.
349. Doctrine and Covenants 128:21; see also Doctrine and Covenants 98:12.
350. See 1 Kings 19:12; 1 Nephi 17:45; Doctrine and Covenants 85:6.
351. Helaman 5:30.
352. Mark 4:38–41; emphasis added.
353. Ether 12:6.
354. 2 Timothy 1:7.
355. 2 Timothy 1:7.
356. "Willing," *Oxford Dictionary of English*, 2030.
357. Doctrine and Covenants 20:77; emphasis added.
358. 2 Nephi 31:13; Moroni 7:6, 9; 10:4.
359. Nelson, "Let God Prevail."
360. See Alma 32:2–43.
361. Alma 32:27.
362. Alma 32:28.
363. Alma 32:37.
364. Alma 32:28.
365. See Alma 32:32.
366. See Alma 33:1.
367. See Alma 33:2–11.
368. Alma 33:2.
369. Alma 33:2.
370. Alma 33:3.
371. Alma 33:4–8.
372. Alma 33:8.
373. Alma 33:9.
374. Alma 33:10.
375. Alma 33:11.
376. Alma 33:11.
377. See Alma 33:19–22.
378. Alma 33:19.
379. Alma 37:46.
380. Ashton, "Peace: A Triumph of Principles"; emphasis added.
381. See Doctrine and Covenants 46:13–14.
382. Malachi 3:10.
383. See Bible Dictionary, "Repentance," 760.
384. Mosiah 3:19.
385. 1 Corinthians 2:16.
386. Doctrine and Covenants 64:10.
387. Luke 10:1–4.
388. Luke 10:5.
389. Alma 37:6.
390. Act 10:38.

391. Oaks, "Small and Simple Things."
392. See "The Family: A Proclamation to the World."
393. Uchtdorf, "Of Things That Matter Most."
394. Nelson, Footnote 18, in Renlund, "Unwavering Commitment to Jesus Christ."
395. Covenants are often described as two-way agreements, willingly entered by both parties. This definition is accurate, but it is incomplete. Covenants also form a new relationship between two individuals—in this case, between our Heavenly Father and us. That new relationship governs what we do, how we interact with and feel about each other, and what we expect from one another.
396. See Doctrine and Covenants 20:77, 79.
397. "Remember," *Oxford Dictionary of English,* 1502.
398. Marder, "The Importance of Remembering"; emphasis added.
399. Mahr and Csibra, "Witnessing, Remembering, and Testifying," 428–443; emphasis added.
400. Mosiah 18:9.
401. Multiple scriptures affirm that all things point us to and remind us of Christ. (See 2 Nephi 11:4; Mosiah 3:15; Alma 30:44; Helaman 8:24; Moses 6:63).
402. See Moses 1:39.
403. See John 5:30; 6:38–40.
404. 2 Nephi 2:11.
405. See Hebrews 12:2.
406. Doctrine and Covenants 122:7.
407. Alma 34:16.
408. Bujnowski, *Discovering Your Temple Insights,* 199.
409. See Alma 36:28–29; 38:7; Helaman 6–7.
410. Mark 4:38.
411. Mark 4:39.
412. Matthew 8:26.
413. 1 Nephi 11:17.
414. John 15:13.
415. Doctrine and Covenants 19:16–18.
416. Doctrine and Covenants 45:3–5.
417. Deuteronomy 6:12.
418. Doctrine and Covenants 20:29.
419. Matthew Struthers, conversation with the authors, December 4, 2024.
420. Matthew 10:22; see also Matthew 24:13; Mark 13:13.
421. Center on the Developing Child, The Science of Resilience (InBrief), 2015.
422. Self-efficacy is a person's belief in their ability to successfully perform and accomplish specific tasks or goals.
423. Self-regulation is a person's ability to control their thoughts, emotions, and behaviors in a way that allows them to accomplish their goals.
424. See Romans 8:28.
425. Doctrine and Covenants 121:8.
426. 1 Peter 2:20.

427. Maxwell, "If Thou Endure It Well."
428. Moroni 7:45; see also 1 Corinthians 13:4.
429. Maxwell, "If Thou Endure It Well."
430. Tim Taggart, "In the Strength of the Lord," personal communication to the authors, March 17, 2013.
431. Doctrine and Covenants 76:50–70 contain a description of those who enter the celestial kingdom. The greatest number of verses are dedicated to this kingdom of glory. Verse 50 is an introduction, verses 51–53 provide the three requirements, and verses 54–70 provide a detailed description of the blessings celestial beings receive.
432. Doctrine and Covenants 76:51.
433. Doctrine and Covenants 76:51–52. The doctrine of Christ is to have faith on Jesus, repent, be baptized, receive the gift of the Holy Ghost, and endure to the end. These items are essentially what is described in verses 51–52.
434. Doctrine and Covenants 76:53.
435. Doctrine and Covenants 76:53. Being sealed by the Holy Spirit of Promise is different than receiving the marriage sealing ordinance. Being sealed by the Holy Spirit of Promise means that the person's faith and life—what he or she has become—has been ratified by the Holy Ghost.
436. According to Elder David A. Bednar, "The Holy Spirit of Promise is the ratifying power of the Holy Ghost. When sealed by the Holy Spirit of Promise, an ordinance, vow, or covenant is binding on earth and in heaven. (See Doctrine and Covenants 132:7) Receiving this 'stamp of approval' from the Holy Ghost is the result of faithfulness, integrity, and steadfastness in honoring gospel covenants" (David A. Bednar, "Ye Must Be Born Again," *Ensign*, May 2007).
437. See Romans 8:28.
438. Moroni 8:3.
439. Angie Vach, "Our Family's Foundation of Hope Amid Grief," Temple Insights Blog, December 28, 2022.
440. James 5:11.
441. See Alma 19:6.
442. Nelson, "Joy and Spiritual Survival."
443. *Children's Songbook,* 60.
444. *Children's Songbook,* 60.
445. Psalm 72:17.
446. Psalm 106:1; see also Psalms 107:1; 118:1; 136:1.
447. Psalm 111:3.
448. Psalm 145:13.
449. See Moroni 7:40–42.
450. Richter, "On the Phenomenon of Sudden Death in Animals and Man," 12–16.
451. Ether 12:6.
452. Jessica Giles, email to the authors, December 11, 2024. This sister missionary is now a mother of three children and has been cancer-free since receiving her treatments.
453. Maxwell, "In Him All Things Hold Together."
454. 2 Timothy 4:7.

455. 1 John 2:9–10.
456. Matthew 5:14–16.
457. See Moroni 7:48.
458. Doctrine and Covenants 81:5.
459. Kimball, "Small Acts of Service"; emphasis added.
460. Romans 12:1.
461. Psalm 23:3.
462. Matthew 22:36–40; emphasis added.
463. See Luke 10:29–37.
464. Miller, "New Testament, Episode 33: Romans 1–6, Part 2," timestamp 22:56; emphasis added.
465. John 14:15.
466. John 15:12–13; emphasis added.
467. John 5:30.
468. Luke 22:42.
469. Matthew 5:45; emphasis added.
470. Doctrine and Covenants 121:8; see also Mosiah 24:14–15.
471. Genesis 24:1.
472. Dallin H. Oaks, "He Heals the Heavy Laden."
473. Jeremiah 8:22.
474. 2 Nephi 11:4; emphasis added.
475. Romans 8:17.
476. 2 Nephi 25:23.
477. 1 Corinthians 10:13.
478. Maxwell, "Grounded, Rooted, Established, and Settled,.
479. 3 Nephi 18:16, 24; emphasis added.
480. Alonso, "Doing the Right Thing at the Right Time, without Delay."
481. Monson, "Our Brothers' Keepers," 39.
482. Valiant class is a program in The Church of Jesus Christ of Latter-day Saints for girls ages eight to eleven.
483. Allison Vander Meiden, email to Aaron Bujnowski, January 9, 2011.
484. Ibid.
485. 1 John 1:7–8.
486. Mark 16:15.
487. Catherine Bass, personal communication to the authors, December 8, 2024.
488. Isaiah 2:5.
489. John 15:9.
490. 2 Nephi 31.20; emphasis added.
491. Mosiah 5:2; see also Alma 19:33.
492. Alma 5:14.
493. Christofferson, "When Thou Art Converted."
494. See Alma 23:6.
495. Daniel 3:17–18; emphasis added.
496. Christofferson, "Born Again."

497. See 2 Corinthians 5:17.
498. Scott, "Full Conversion Brings Happiness."
499. Christofferson, "Why the Church."
500. Bednar, "Converted Unto the Lord."
501. See Matthew 19:16–22; Mark 10:17–22; Luke 18:18–23.
502. Holland, "Israel, Israel, God Is Calling."
503. Moses 1:39.
504. 3 Nephi 12:24.
505. Ephesians 4:13.
506. Bernards, "'This Whole Journey Was Sacred,'" 134.
507. Maxwell, "In Him All Things Hold Together."
508. Holland, "Be Ye Therefore Perfect, Eventually."
509. David Hixon, "Faith to Be Healed," email to the authors, December 4, 2024.
510. Moroni 10:32.
511. 2 Corinthians 12:9; Ether 12:26; Doctrine and Covenants 18:31.
512. Isiah 41:10; emphasis added.
513. 2 Nephi 26:33.
514. Jeremiah 31:3.
515. Kearon, "God's Intent Is to Bring You Home."
516. See Luke 22:54–62.
517. See Luke 15:17.
518. Isaiah 43:1–3; emphasis added.
519. Isaiah 61:1–4.
520. Isaiah 61:3.
521. Enos 1:2.
522. Alma 36:10.
523. Acts 22:6–7.
524. Enos 1:4.
525. Alma 36:12.
526. Acts 9:6.
527. Acts 22:17–18.
528. Enos 1:3.
529. Alma 36:17.
530. Acts 26:16.
531. Enos 1:4.
532. Alma 36:18.
533. Acts 22:8, 10.
534. Enos 1:6.
535. Alma 36:27.
536. Acts 9:29.
537. Enos 1:4, 8.
538. Alma 36:30.
539. Acts 22:10; 26:19.
540. Enos 1:15.

541. Alma 36:28–29.
542. Acts 26:22–23.
543. Enos 1:26.
544. Alma 36:27.
545. Acts 26:21–22.
546. Enos 1:9–10.
547. Alma 36:24.
548. Acts 26:20.
549. Enos 1:11.
550. Alma 36:19–20.
551. 2 Timothy 4:7.

WORKS CITED

Alonso, Jose L. "Doing the Right Thing at the Right Time, without Delay." *Ensign,* Nov. 2011.

Ashton, Marvin J. "Peace: A Triumph of Principles." *Peace.* Deseret Book, 1988.

Bednar, David A. "A Reservoir of Living Water." *BYU Speeches,* February 4, 2007.

Bednar, David A. "Converted Unto the Lord." *Ensign,* Nov. 2012.

Bednar, David A. "Special Witnesses of the Name of Christ." *Religious Educator* 12, no. 2, 2011.

Bednar, David A. "Ye Must Be Born Again." *Ensign,* May 2007.

Benson, Ezra Taft. "Beware of Pride." *Ensign*, May 1989.

Benson, Ezra Taft. *Teachings of Ezra Taft Benson*. Bookcraft, 1988.

Bernards, Julia Campbell. "'This whole journey was sacred': Latter-day Saint Parents' Process in Coming to Accept a Transgender Child." PhD diss., Brigham Young University, 2022. *BYU Scholars Archive.* Publication no. 9809.

Bujnowski Aaron and Bujnowski, Julie. *Discovering Your Temple Insights*. Cedar Fort Publishing & Media, 2023.

Center on the Developing Child. *The Science of Resilience (InBrief).* Harvard University, 2015. https://developingchild.harvard.edu/science/key-concepts/resilience/.

Christofferson, D. Todd. "Born Again." *Ensign,* May 2008.

Christofferson, D. Todd. "Our Relationship with God." *Liahona,* April 2022.

Christofferson, D. Todd. "When Thou Art Converted." *Ensign*, May 2004.

Christofferson, D. Todd. "Why the Church." *Ensign*, November 2015.

Clark, J. Reuben. Conference Report, 1953.

Edenberg, Howard J, and Tatiana Foroud. "Genetics and Alcoholism." *Nature Reviews Gastroenterol & Hepatology* (2013): 487–94. doi: 10.1038/nrgastro.2013.86.

Eyring, Henry B. "Gifts of the Spirit for Hard Times," *Ensign*, June 2007.

Fowler, James W. *Stages of Faith: The Psychology of Human Development and the Quest for Meaning.* HarperCollins, 1995.

General Handbook, Serving in The Church of Jesus Christ of Latter-day Saints, Gospel Library.

Hales, Brook P. "Mortality Works." *Ensign,* November 2004.

Holland, Jeffrey R. "Abide in Me." *Ensign*, May 2004.

Holland, Jeffrey R. "Be Ye Therefore Perfect, Eventually." *Ensign*, November 2007.

Holland, Jeffrey R. "I Am He," *Liahona,* November 2024.

Holland, Jeffrey R. "Israel, Israel, God Is Calling." CES Broadcast, September 10, 2012.

Hymns. The Church of Jesus Christ of Latter-day Saints, 1985.

Kearon, Patrick. "God's Intent Is to Bring You Home." *Liahona*, May 2024.

Kimball, Spencer W. "Small Acts of Service." *Ensign*, December 1974.

Kimball, Spencer W. *Tragedy or Destiny?* Deseret Book, 1977.

Mahr, J.B. and Gergely Csibra. "Witnessing, Remembering, and Testifying: Why the Past Is Special for Human Beings." *Perspectives on Psychological Science* 15, no. 2 (2020): 428–443. https://doi.org/10.1177/1745691619879167.

Marder, Eve. "The importance of remembering." *eLife*. vol. 6 e30599. August 14, 2017. doi:10.7554 / eLife.30599.

Maxwell, Neal A. "Grounded, Rooted, Established, and Settled." BYU Speeches, September 15, 1981.

Maxwell, Neal A. "If Thou Endure It Well." BYU Speeches, December 4, 1984.

Maxwell, Neal A. "In Him All Things Hold Together." BYU Speec hes, March 31, 1991.

Maxwell, Neal A. "Jesus of Nazareth, Savior and King." *Ensign,* April 1976.

McConkie, Bruce R. "The Purifying Power of Gethsemane." *Ensign,* May 1985.

McKay, David O., in Conference Report, April 1959.

McLaren, Brian D. *Faith After Doubt.* St. Martin's Essentials, 2021.

McLaren, Brian D. "Your Faith Isn't Broken." *Faith Matters.* Podcast. September 23, 2023.

Miller, Adam S. "New Testament, Episode 33: Romans 1–6, Part 2," *Follow Him,* podcast with Hank Smith and John Bytheway, August 7–13, 2023. https://followhim.co/wp-content/uploads/2023/08/NT-33–Dr.-Adam-Miller-Romans-1–6–followHIM-Podcast-SHOW-NOTES.pdf.

Monson, Thomas S. "Our Brothers' Keepers." *Ensign*, June 1998.

Monson, Thomas S. "Status Report on Missionary Work: A Conversation with Elder Thomas S. Monson, Chairman of the Missionary Committee of the Council of the Twelve." *Ensign*, November 1977.

Monson, Thomas S. "The Master's Blueprint." *Ensign*, January 2006.

Nelson, Russel M. and Wendy W. Nelson, "Hope of Israel" [worldwide youth devotional, June 3, 2018], Gospel Library.

Nelson, Russell M. "Choices for Eternity." Worldwide Devotional for Young Adults, May 15, 2022.

Nelson, Russell M. "Joy and Spiritual Survival." *Ensign* or *Liahona,* November 2016.

Nelson, Russell. M. "Let God Prevail." *Liahona,* November 30, 2024.

Nelson, Russell M. "The Answer Is Always Jesus Christ." *Liahona,* April 2023.

Oaks, Dallin H. "He Heals the Heavy Laden." *Ensign,* November 2006.

Oaks, Dallin H. "Sins and Mistakes." BYU Speeches, August 16, 1994.

Packer, Boyd K. "Prayer and Promptings." *Ensign,* November 2009.

Packer, Boyd K. "The Edge of the Light." BYU Speeches, March 4, 1990.

Packer, Boyd K. "The Instrument of Your Mind and the Foundation of Your Character." BYU Speeches, February 2, 2003.

Preach My Gospel: A Guide to Sharing the Gospel of Jesus Christ. The Church of Jesus Christ of Latter-day Saints, 2023.

Oaks, Dallin H. "Small and Simple Things." *Ensign,* May 2018.

Renlund, Dale G. "Unwavering Commitment to Jesus Christ." *Ensign,* November 2019.

Richter, Curt P. "On the Phenomenon of Sudden Death in Animals and Man." *Psychiatric Research Reports*, no. 8, 1957. https://www.aipro.info/wp/wp-content/uploads/2017/08/phenomena_sudden_death.pdf.

Robbins, Lynn G. "Until Seventy Times Seven." *Ensign,* May 2018.

Sabin, Gary B. "Hallmarks of Happiness." *Liahona*, November 2023.

Scott, Richard G. "Finding the Joy in Life." *Ensign,* May 1996.

Scott Richard G. "Full Conversion Brings Happiness." *Ensign*, May 2002.

Smith, Joseph. *History of the Church*. Deseret Book, 1980.

Smith, Joseph. *Lectures on Faith* (1835).

Taylor, Jennie. *Life Is Incredibly Unfair, In Our Favor*, (video). The Church of Jesus Christ of Latter-day Saints. https://youtu.be/HSFD3jtJV30.

Teaching in the Savior's Way. The Church of Jesus Christ of Latter-day Saints, 2022.

"The Family: A Proclamation to the World." *Ensign*. November 1995.

The Living Christ: The Testimony of the Apostles. The Church of Jesus Christ of Latter-day Saints, January 1, 2000.

Tiwari, Ashish. "How Do Seeds Know They Have to Grow Upwards Against Gravity?" *Science ABC*, 21 May, 2017.

Topics and Questions. The Church of Jesus Christ of Latter-day Saints.

Uchtdorf, Dieter F. "Of Things That Matter Most." *Ensign*, November 2010.

"What is Alcohol Use Disorder?" *Bowles Center for Alcohol Studies*. University of North Carolina at Chapel Hill. https://www.med.unc.edu/alcohol/education-prevention/alcoholism-and-alcohol-abuse/alcoholism/.

Wilcox, Brad. "Book of Mormon, Episode 40: 3 Nephi 12–16, Part 2." *Follow Him Podcast with Hank Smith and John Bytheway*. Podcast transcript, September 30–October 6, 2024. Accessed November 27, 2024.

Wirthlin, Joseph B. "Shall He Find Faith on the Earth?" *Ensign*, November 2002.

ABOUT THE AUTHORS

Aaron and Julie Bujnowski met in the high school band when they were living in Nashville, Tennessee. Aaron was a Church member, and when they met, Julie was not a member. She began to attend Church meetings and activities with him, eventually joining the Church in 1989. Aaron served as a missionary in the Chile Concepción Mission from 1990 to 1992, and they married shortly after he returned in 1992 in the Atlanta Georgia Temple.

Julie and Aaron are the authors of *Discovering Your Temple Insights* (Cedar Fort, 2023). Described as "Come, Follow Me for the temple," their book includes rich information and a simple framework that helps readers learn more from the temple. The book has helped new and experienced members improve their ability to gain personal temple insights and connect with their Savior in His house.

Julie has an associate of science degree in general studies and a BS in professional studies from BYU–Idaho. Aaron has BS and MS degrees in chemical engineering from BYU–Provo, an MBA from the University of Texas at Austin, and a DSc in healthcare leadership from the University of Alabama at Birmingham.

Julie and Aaron are the parents of two adult children, and they live in Frisco, Texas.